John P. Braun
Feb 2010.

FIRST COMES
LOVE?

Mary and Joey

Sitting in a tree,

K-I-S-S-I-N-G.

First comes love,

Then comes marriage,

Then comes Mary

With a baby carriage.

FIRST COMES LOVE?

THE CHANGING FACE OF MARRIAGE

JOHN C. MORRIS

THE PILGRIM PRESS · CLEVELAND

TO SUSAN,

with whom I have journeyed in companionship and joy

The Pilgrim Press, 700 Prospect Avenue East, Cleveland, Ohio 44115-1100
thepilgrimpress.com
© 2007 by John C. Morris

All rights reserved. Published 2007

Printed in the United States of America on acid-free paper.

09 08 07 06   5 4 3 2 1

Library of Congress Cataloging-in-Publication Data

Morris, John C., 1943–
  First comes love? : the ever-changing face of marriage / John C. Morris.
    p. cm.
  ISBN 978-0-8298-1755-3 (alk. paper)
  1. Marriage—Religious aspects—Christianity. 2. Marriage—History.
I. Title.

BV835.M68 2007
261.8'358109—dc22   2006036276

CONTENTS

✤ ACKNOWLEDGMENTS ✤ 7

✤ PROLOGUE: The Changing Face of Marriage ✤ 9

1 ✤ HOW DIFFERENT CULTURES PORTRAY RELATIONSHIPS: ✤ 11
The Creation Stories of Olympus and Eden

2 ✤ MARRIAGE WITHIN ONE'S CROWD ✤ 14
Endogamy: Isaac and Rebekah · Polygamy and Concubinage: Jacob and Leah and Rachel, Zilpah and Bilhah · Levirate Marriage · Arranged Marriages · Resistance to Mixed Marriages · Alternatives: Jonah and Ruth

3 ✤ MARRIAGE FOR POLITICAL PURPOSES ✤ 35

4 ✤ MARRIAGE FOR PROCREATION ✤ 40

5 ✤ FOUR REVOLUTIONARY MARRIAGE TRADITIONS FROM THE CHURCH ✤ 44
Slaves and Citizens Can Marry · Celibacy · Women Are Equal to Men · Lifelong Commitment · A Brief Summary

6 ✤ WHAT MAKES A MARRIAGE VALID? ✤ 55
Mutual Consent · Consummation · Validation by an Outside Authority

7 ✤ MARRIAGE AS A SECULAR CONTRACT ✤ 66

8 ✤ MARRIAGE AS A SACRED COVENANT ✤ 69

9 ✤ BETROTHAL ✤ 73

10 ✤ MODERN MARRIAGE ✤ 77
Unhitching Marriage from Property and Procreation · Women's Equality · Marrying for Love · Marrying for Happiness · Ending Marriage through Divorce

11 ✤ MARRIAGE FOR COMPANIONSHIP ✤ 94

12 ✤ A CONCLUDING MARRIAGE CHECKLIST ✤ 98

13 ✤ EDEN REVISITED ✤ 103

✤ EPILOGUE: Sketches for a New Portrait of Marriage ✤ 108

✤ APPENDIX A: Questions for Reflection and Discussion ✤ 115

✤ APPENDIX B: Marriage Quiz ✤ 118

✤ NOTES ✤ 123

✤ BIBLIOGRAPHY ✤ 126

ACKNOWLEDGMENTS

The idea for this book has been germinating for several years. In 2004, I received a study grant through the Pastoral Enrichment Project, which is sponsored by Episcopal Divinity School (EDS) in Cambridge, Massachusetts, and by the Episcopal Diocese of Vermont. With the resources provided by the grant, I was able to spend time at EDS and do most of the research and some of the writing for the manuscript for this book. I am very grateful to Chris Carr at EDS and to Susan Ohlidahl from the Diocese of Vermont, who facilitated the grant for me. Also, I appreciate the helpfulness of the library staff at EDS during the time I was doing my research.

Many colleagues in the Diocese of Vermont helped me clarify my thinking on the topic of the history of marriage. Lee Crawford, Anne Brown, Gordon Bardos, and Steve Swayne were especially helpful. The bishop of the Diocese, Tom Ely, was always very encouraging and supportive of my work on this book.

The parishioners and vestry of St. Martin's Episcopal Church in Fairlee, Vermont, where I currently serve as rector, have been consistently kind in providing me with time away from the parish to engage in study projects, and I am grateful for their support.

June and Jim Hagen, long-time friends, have always encouraged my writing activities and, in this most recent project, they were steadfastly enthusiastic.

I gratefully acknowledge permission to reprint lyrics from Loretta Lynn's song "The Pill" © 1975 Loretta Lynn; and from "Love and Marriage," words by Sammy Cahn, music by James Van Heusen, copyright ©1955 (renewed) Barton Music Corp. and Cahn Music Company. All rights reserved. Used by permission. I am also grateful to Stephanie Coontz, director of public education for the Council on Contemporary Families, and a faculty member at Evergreen State College in Olympia Washington, for use of "A Pop Quiz on Marriage," from the *New York Times* op-ed section, Sunday, February 19, 2006. Most of the information for the quiz comes from her book *Marriage, a History: How Love Conquered Marriage* (New York: Viking Press, 2005).

In the Fall of 2005, I was fortunate to attend a conference where Dr. Marvin Ellison of Bangor Theological Seminary was the keynote speaker. During the conference, I had the opportunity to tell him about my research and writing, and he encouraged me to send my manuscrpt to Ulrike Guthrie, his editor at The Pilgrim Press. I appreciate his help in making that contact and his ongoing support for this project.

The task of getting a manuscript ready for publication as a book is a very new activity for me. With the magnanimous and skilled help of Ulrike Guthrie, and the competent work of Kris Firth, copy editor for the publisher, I was able to accomplish this task in a surprisingly enjoyable manner. I thank them for making that possible.

Above all, I am grateful to my wife, Susan, who read all the drafts, alerted me to some errors in spelling and grammar, and challenged me to make the text as accessible as possible to people who might read it. What a blessing it is for me to have her as a companion on our particular marriage journey.

PROLOGUE

The Changing Face of Marriage

People have been marrying for thousands of years. In this book, I invite you to look at this aged institution and see how it has changed and changed and changed again. We hear much discussion these days about "traditional marriage," as if there is a single, unchanging tradition of marriage that goes back to the beginning of history. However, a careful study reveals that marriage has been a very elastic institution. Unlike the ancient dinosaurs, who could not adapt to new conditions, marriage has been malleable enough to be shaped and reshaped by us into a variety of forms.

Marriage traditions are many layered. The most recent picture is different from the ones that lie beneath it. Humans have indeed changed many of the ways they have bound themselves together in marriage.

I invite you in this book on a brief exploration of twenty-one of these various layers and traditions. I will move quickly, somewhat like a guide in an art museum who wants the visitors to get a brief glimpse of the entire collection without pausing too long in any one gallery. I will comment on the broad strokes of the various portraits of marriage that have been created in the past but will not linger too long on any one of them. The bibliography at the end of the book suggests where to find more detailed treatment of the various traditions that lie underneath our contemporary version of marriage. Finally, in the epilogue, I make a few sketches for a new portrait of marriage based on my own analysis of this history and my own vision of what might emerge in the future.

I hope that what follows will help us transcend some of the overblown rhetoric and heated emotions that characterize our discussions of marriage. If we can see again all of the variegated layers of paint that are under our present portrait and understand why these changes have occurred, I think we will appreciate better where we have been in the past, where we might be headed in the future, and how God has been intimately involved in this long and fascinating history.

As I invite you to look at the evolution of marriage, I want to be clear about my own point of view. I grew up in the midwestern part of the United States in the 1950s. My father died when I was four years old and my mother never remarried. In 1966, I married my high school sweetheart, and we moved to the East Coast to live and work and go to school. My wife, Susan, and I have three grown children, two of whom are married. I was ordained as an Episcopal priest in 1968 and have served several small parishes in the Diocese of Vermont since 1971. While working part-time in these churches, I earned my living as an elementary school teacher in four different schools before retiring from the classroom in 1999. All of these experiences have shaped the way that I see marriage, just as your experiences shape the way you see marriage.

Though I speak only from my own limited experience and study of the traditions that lie under our contemporary version of marriage, I hope you will find here something helpful to the very important discussion about the ever-changing institution of marriage.

I

HOW DIFFERENT CULTURES PORTRAY RELATIONSHIPS

The Creation Stories of Olympus and Eden

One way of gaining insight into how people understand human relationships is by looking at their creation stories. Out of the many, many such stories found in cultures all over the world, I think one ancient story is especially interesting. It comes from Greece.

The ancient Greeks believed that the gods resided on Mt. Olympus and from that lofty perch created human beings. Their creation story is quite tragic. It seems that Prometheus took pity on primitive humankind and stole fire from the gods to give to humans. Zeus was so angered by this that he chained Prometheus to Mount Caucasus, where an eagle came every day to tear at his liver, which then grew back again every night.

While Prometheus was being constantly "de-livered," Zeus ordered his blacksmith, Hephaestus, to create the first woman, an evil being whom all men would desire. Hephaestus got to work and, from earth and water, created Pandora, which means "all gifts." She was beautiful, artistic, and cunning. She was given to Prometheus' brother, Epimetheus, and brought with her a box containing special gifts for humanity. When she lifted the lid of the box, out came all the world's vices and sins and diseases and troubles. And the rest, as the ancient Greeks would have said, is history.

This old Greek story is just one of many stories from around the world that we could explore to see how a particular group of people envisioned human relationships. The story of Pandora seems to be especially egregious in terms of its negative view of women, which just adds more sadness to its already tragic view of human identity and destiny.

The Hebrews had a very different creation story. The Creator fashioned the world and humans for delight and pleasure. The gifts and blessings given to humans were given out of divine love, not out of Zeusian spite. According to Genesis 1, after each day of creation, relishing what had been created and nodding happily, God shouted, "Tov!" (meaning, "that's good!"). At the climax of creation, God created male and female to be equal partners as God launched this new project called "humankind." At the end of that day, God sang out joyfully, "Tov meov!" ("that's *very* good!").

In the Greek story, the woman is created as punishment. By contrast, in the Hebrew story, the woman is created as a companion to the man. The first thing the Hebrew Creator-God declares as being "not good" is that the first human was alone: "It is not good that the man should be alone. I will make him a helper as his partner." (Gen. 2:18) In other words, God saw that isolation is terrible and human aloneness is something from which God wants to deliver us.

So when I think about the history of marriage, I don't turn first to the Hebrew creation story. I don't interpret that story to be fundamentally about marriage. I see it as a painting of the primal couple for whom companionship is the purpose of their being. Humans were created for relationship, mirroring the very Being of God, whom we Christians imagine in our notion of the Trinity as being ultimate Relationship. In that profound image of separateness-in-unity and unity-in-separateness, we see ourselves and our destiny. We are meant for community and relationship. Looking back through the mists of myth and history, we see the divine desire to have humans overcome isolation as they set out as partners on the great adventure of becoming children of God.

If I were painting a picture of the primal couple, I would not put wedding clothes on them. As a matter of fact, the original artist put no clothes on them. The point of the story was not to get them married but to get them going on their adventure. No wedding gowns, no tuxedos. No vows, no certificates. Just two naked people, leaning on each other, trying to make sense of their surroundings and the meaning of their lives. Two people, trying to understand their relationship to God while also trying to figure out how to be companions to each other.

We will return to that primal couple in Eden at the end of the book. For now, it seems important to leave them in Eden and turn to the couple who, in our Judeo-Christian tradition, are the ones who are first described as being "married."

❋ 2 ❋

MARRIAGE WITHIN ONE'S CROWD

ENDOGAMY: ISAAC AND REBEKAH

> Isaac went out in the evening to walk in the field; and looking up, he saw camels coming. And Rebekah looked up, and when she saw Isaac, she slipped quickly from the camel and . . . she took her veil and covered herself. And the servant told Isaac all the things he had done. Then Isaac brought her into his mother Sarah's tent. He took Rebekah and she became his wife; and he loved her. (Gen. 24:63–64, 65b–67a)

The first true portrait of marriage in Hebrew Scripture is the marriage of Isaac and Rebekah. There are many marriages that preceded this one, but this is the first one to catch the storyteller's full attention. Other marriages are either alluded to or dealt with in one quick verse, but this marriage gets an entire chapter in Genesis. It has many layers of drama, is told with great sensitivity, and ends with the first biblical occurrence of someone being described as loving a spouse.

Adam and Eve may have discovered they loved each other. Abraham and Sarah, Abraham and Hagar, and then Abraham and Keturah (Gen. 25:1) may have experienced love in their relationships, but if they did, that fact never made it onto the storyteller's radar screen. If we really want to see a full depiction of marriage in the early history of the Hebrew people, we should look at chapter 24 of Genesis. That story, told with reverence and delicacy, reveals much about the tradition of marriage during the time of the biblical patriarchs and matriarchs.

As we glance at the details in this complex portrait, we see some marriage customs very different from our contemporary ones.

First, the reason that Abraham's servant was waiting expectantly by the well way up in Aramnaharaim was that he had to find a wife for Isaac among Abraham's "kindred." Isaac definitely could not be married to the girl next door, who was a Canaanite (Gen. 24:3); because she was not from Isaac's tribe, she would have been out of bounds in terms of marriage. The sociological word to describe this marriage tradition is "endogamy" (marriage within the tribe).

The fact that Rebekah was Isaac's cousin was not an issue for our spiritual ancestors. The important thing was that she was "one of us." She was part of "our crowd," and therefore an appropriate woman for Isaac to marry. The story does say that Rebekah consented to the arrangement (Gen. 24:58), but I would imagine that she was a bright young woman who could see the handwriting on the wall and realized that all of that gold and jewelry sent from Abraham and spread around in her parents' tent meant that the two fathers had more or less closed the deal. So, off she went to meet Isaac for the first time.

But this is not a scene that most contemporary Western Christians repeat in their own marriage arrangements. We no longer follow the tradition of endogamous marriage, although the mentality of keeping marriage within the bounds of "our kind of people" is definitely still with us. For example, in twentieth-century America, forty-one states and territories barred marriage between the races. Similarly, in 1998, a Roman Catholic woman's house in Northern Ireland was set on fire and her children were killed, apparently because she was living with a Protestant. The ghost of Phineas, the priest who slew an Israelite and his Moabite wife (Num. 25:6–8a), still stalks the land, intent on upholding the tradition of keeping marriage within "our crowd."

However much the impulse towards endogamy still exists, the fact is that in our contemporary Western marriage arrangements fathers do not usually send messengers back to the land from which they or their ancestors emigrated. Modern-day fathers and mothers may wish that their son or daughter will find a spouse among their own "kind," but the tradition that requires this practice has mostly fallen by the wayside. Furthermore, it is no longer a tradition that the young woman must be a virgin (Gen. 24:16). This topic of the necessary virginity of the bride—but not the groom (!)—will resurface in several later chapters; at this point it seems important simply to note it as one part of the ancient tradition of endogamous marriage.

In this kind of endogamous marriage, love was clearly not a requirement, though sometimes a happy serendipity. We'll keep an eye open for this thing called "love" as we move through this history, but it won't take up much of the canvas until we get to chapter 10 on the modern traditions of marriage.

So we need to move on to the next biblical tradition, the next layer of this portrait of marriage. It's the complex story of Jacob and his two wives . . . and their two handmaidens.

POLYGAMY AND CONCUBINAGE:
Jacob and Leah and Rachel, Zilpah and Bilhah

> In the evening, Laban took his daughter Leah and brought her to Jacob; and he went in to her. . . . When morning came, it was Leah! And Jacob said to Laban, "What is this you have done to me? Did I not serve you for Rachel? Why then have you deceived me?" Laban said, "This is not done in our country—giving the younger before the firstborn." (Gen. 29:23, 25–26)

This next portrait of biblical marriage needs a big canvas, for there are lots and lots of people in it. The picture that I see is rather like a photograph of a famous athletic team. If each character had a number on his or her shirt, it would really help us sort out who is who in this very complex story.

Jacob, of course, would be Number 1. His marriages are at the center of the story. He is the star of this team, the one who outwitted his dimwit brother in order to secure the favored place in the generation after Isaac. He is the child of promise, the superstar, the one on whom the future of the tribe depends. Definitely, #1.

Rachel, "graceful and beautiful" (Gen. 29:17b), stands to Jacob's right in this group picture. She is wearing jersey #2. She is the woman Jacob loved first and, as this grand soap opera developed, she is also the one he loved the most. Next to Rachel, wearing uniform #4, is her handmaid, Bilhah.

On Jacob's left, the woman with the lovely eyes (Gen. 29:17a) is Leah, who is Rachel's older sister. She is wearing uniform #3. If you look closely at Leah and Rachel, you can see that the eyes of both sisters contain traces of steely determination and also signs of some long-harbored resentments. It has not been a bed of roses for these two women. Next to Leah is her handmaid, Zilpah, wearing a big #5 on her chest.

In front of Jacob and his two wives (Rachel and Leah) and two concubines (Zilpah and Bilhah)—that's right, a subplot in this story is the cultural acceptance of concubinage—are thirteen children. In front of Jacob, wearing a beautiful new multicolored uniform with long sleeves, is Joseph. He has a big star on the front of his shirt, signifying his status as the favored son. Joseph is looking straight at us, with a somewhat smug expression on his young face. Jacob's two hands rest firmly on Joseph's thin shoulders.

Next to Joseph is his little brother, Benjamin, wearing the smallest uniform of all. The rest of the children are arrayed a bit randomly in terms of their uniform numbers, but each child is standing in front of his or her mother. The child who probably catches our attention first, after we have looked at the big star on Joseph's chest and have noted Jacob's large hands on Joseph's shoulders, is the pretty girl standing somewhat shyly in front of Leah. This is Dinah, the only girl among twelve boys. It's difficult to see her because she is partially obscured by the tall and muscular body of her older brother Reuben, who is taller than their mother and almost as tall as Jacob. Kneeling in front of Reuben and Dinah are Simeon and Levi and Judah. Reclining on the ground, in poses similar to some of those old baseball players who were in the front of the team photograph, are Issachar and Zebulon.

On the outer edges of the picture, with facial expressions that seem to be somewhat withdrawn and uninterested, are Zilpah's two children, Gad and Asher, and Bilhah's two children, Dan and Napthtali.

Oh, the stories that could be told about this family! Deceit, passionate love, jealousy, double-crossing, rape, revenge. It's a story that rivals Hollywood's Godfather films and has almost as much violence and scheming as anything dreamt up by Francis Ford Coppola.

The saga of "Godfather" Jacob and his family occupies the entire last half of the book of Genesis. It takes eleven chapters to get from creation to Abraham and Sarah, then another thirteen chapters to get to the marriage of Isaac and Rebekah. After that, for the next twenty-five chapters, it's all about Jacob and his wives, concubines, and children, with a brief side trip through the sibling rivalry of Esau and Jacob. But that little excursion into the lives of the two brothers is definitely worth it. It shows us what lies ahead. Talk about scheming and manipulation! Esau: all brawn and very little brains. Jacob: just the opposite.

When we finally get to the scene in which Jacob is deceived by Laban—the old "switcheroo-of-the-daughters" trick—we have to chuckle a bit because we have seen this before. Doesn't Jacob have any sense of irony as he gets mad at Laban on account of Laban's deceit? Hey, Jacob, remember the scene in your father's tent? The old "let's-pull-the-wool-over-dad's-eyes-and-get-his-blessing" trick? Jacob gets angry because of Laban's deceit. But we've been here before, haven't we? Déjà vu all over again.

What we have to focus on in this story, though, is the tradition of marriage that is on display. It's still the tradition of endogamy. But now endogamy gets a new and complex twist: polygamy—one man with more than one wife. It's not new in human history and it still is very popular in many parts of the world, including Utah and other parts of the United States, but the fact that it takes up the entire second half of Genesis means that it has real biblical legs. It's a tradition that has as much, if not more, biblical support than any other marriage arrangement.

Yet, for the most part, Western Judeo-Christianity has rejected this tradition. Like many subjects raised in this book, the topic of polygamy, which includes both polygyny (one man with more than one wife) and polyandry (one woman with more than one husband), deserves a big book—or several big books—all to itself. The bibliography lists a few works produced by those who are much more familiar with the history of polygamy than I am, but for our purposes it is important to recall that the original portrait of one man/one woman (Isaac and Rebekah) was very quickly covered up by this huge picture of Jacob and his two wives, two concubines, and thirteen children.

Polygamy was the "in thing" for a long time in biblical history and still manifests itself in a variety of ways, including our contemporary tradition of "serial monogamy" as men and women divorce and remarry with mind-boggling frequency. More about that later. But before moving on to the next very unique marriage tradition in our spiritual history, let's take another long look at that picture of Jacob and his four women. In spite of whatever layers of marriage traditions get added to our portrait, we have to take seriously the fact that deeply rooted in our biblical tradition of marriage is polygamy, or more specifically, endogamous polygamy.

In their appeal to "the biblical model of marriage," today's protectors of "traditional marriage" may not have endogamous polygamy in mind, but if we are honest about the revelation of the book of Genesis, we will find that the portrait of Jacob and his four women dominated the canvas for a long time.

LEVIRATE MARRIAGE

When brothers reside together, and one of them dies and has no son, the wife of the deceased shall not be married outside the family to a stranger. Her husband's brother shall go in to her, taking her in marriage, and performing the duty of a husband's brother to her, and the firstborn whom she bears shall succeed to the name of the deceased brother, so that his name may not be blotted out of Israel. But if the man has no desire to marry his brother's widow, then his brother's widow shall go up to the elders at the gate and say, "My husband's brother refuses to perpetuate his brother's name in Israel; he will not perform the duty of a husband's brother to me." Then the elders of his town shall summon him and speak to him. If he persists, saying, "I have no desire to marry her," then his brother's wife shall go up to him in the presence of the elders, pull his sandal off his foot, spit in his face, and declare, "This is what is done to the man who does not build up his brother's house." Throughout Israel, his family will be known as "the house of him whose sandal was pulled off." (Deut. 25:5–10)

The tradition of levirate marriage ("levirate," from the Latin *levir*, meaning "brother-in-law") was rooted in the desire for a man to perpetuate his name, even if he died childless. This is a tradition that also arose out of a concern to protect widows.

A young widow is almost always in a difficult situation. This was especially true in ancient Israel when it was a necessity that she have a man to protect her and care for her. If there was no son left after the death of her husband, the woman was in a very desperate condition.

The beautiful story told in the Book of Ruth has to do with the same situation described in the Deuteronomy passage. One question raised in that book and in the situation just described is: how can the community prevent widows from becoming vulnerable to poverty? The law of levirate marriage became part of the response and was consistent with the biblical injunction to seek justice for widows.

In a patriarchal tribal society, there is a huge amount of pressure to perpetuate the male family line. The death of a young husband who leaves behind a childless widow is a threat to the tribe.

How will that man's family and name be perpetuated? If there is no male heir, it means the man's name is lost forever. It would be as if he had never existed. The solution to this serious problem was to turn to the man's brother and expect him to do his duty. It kept the family bloodline pure. It kept the marriage in the family. It ensured that the man's name would be preserved. When this all happened, the tribe and its elders were very pleased.

The brother-in-law—let's call him "Moshe"—is in a bit of a pickle, though. He may already be married, so suddenly he has to deal with the inevitable tensions of a polygamous marriage. Or, if he is unmarried, he may already have his eye on Serah, the young maiden in the tent across the way, and thus he would be very disappointed not to marry her. Or, as the law from Deuteronomy explains, he may not really care for his sister-in-law. Even so, Moshe doesn't have much wiggle room on this one. Better follow the tradition and hope for the best.

As I ruminate on this fascinating tradition and try to put myself in Moshe's sandals, I naturally think about my own brother, Skip. He's fifteen months older than I am and he has been married two years longer than I have. Like me, Skip married his high school sweetheart, Kathleen. I have always liked Kathleen. She is salt of the earth. She is funny. She is a hard worker and a dependable friend. She is fiercely devoted to her family. And, most amazing of all, she has put up with my brother for lo, these many years.

I try to imagine what would have happened if the Morris family had been part of a tribal culture and we had grown up as nomads out there on the Nebraska prairie. What would have happened, if, not long after my brother had taken Kathleen for his wife, he had met an untimely end—let's say being trampled to death by a rabid bunch of football fans after the University of Nebraska lost a close game to Oklahoma. What would it have been like for me to have to appear before the elders? What would I have said after Kathleen's opening speech? Would I have married her?

This is just a quick sketch of the unique institution of levirate marriage. It doesn't occupy a big part of our historical portrait, but it does point to an extremely important aspect of marriage—protecting the family property. Intertwined with so many marriage traditions is the crucial question of how to transfer wealth and possessions from one generation to the next. In other words, a major part of the development of marriage traditions is: Who will get "the Stuff?" That topic will be part of the picture for much of the discussion in succeeding chapters. But before dealing with that issue, we need to add a very colorful character to our portrait.

ARRANGED MARRIAGES

"Matchmaker, Matchmaker, make me a match . . ."

The next portrait of marriage shows two men, with drinking glasses raised, toasting each other as they close the deal on a marriage. It's the famous scene from the musical *Fiddler on the Roof*. On the right is Tevye the Milkman, father of Tzeitel. On the left, is Lazer Wolf the Butcher, a widower who wants to marry Tzeitel, even though he is much, much older than she is.

The person who has brought these two men to the table is Yenta the Matchmaker. She moves in and out of the story, not as a dominant person, but as a very symbolic figure. She symbolizes the long and important tradition of arranged marriages. Marriage in ancient Israel and in many cultures around the world and in the fictional town of Anatevka was an agreement between two heads of families, not between two individuals who were in love. The tension between those two different models of marriage is what gives the Fiddler story its drama and poignancy.

Early in the Fiddler story, Tevye's three older daughters sing the lilting and energetic song: "Matchmaker, Matchmaker, make me a match, find me a find, catch me a catch . . . ," dramatizing the fact that their marriages are not within their own control. Their father, with the help of Yenta, will determine what happens to them in the future.

It would be interesting to take a long side trip into the gallery that shows portraits of professional matchmakers throughout the ages, but that would take us too far away from our essential purpose here. With the image of Tevye and Lazer Wolf in our minds, though, it seems useful to consider one highly important match that is crucial in our spiritual history: the match made between Joseph and Mary of Nazareth.

According to tradition, Joseph was an older man, possibly a widower, while Mary, like Tevye's daughter Tzeitel, was very young. So there we have a fascinating portrait to add to our collection: a Lazer Wolfish Joseph negotiating with Mary's father, who resembles the Broadway show version of Tevye. Important here is that Jesus of Nazareth was the product of an arranged marriage. Two men decided the fate of a young woman and her future progeny. This tradition of arranged marriages is not adhered to in most Western cultures today, but there it is, front and center, in the drama of the life of Jesus.

The underlying premise of arranged marriages, of course, was not just about getting two people together for the purposes of matrimony, but to ensure that property would be transferred in acceptable ways to the next generation. Even in peasant societies, whether in fictional Anatevka or in ancient Galilee, there still was concern about the Stuff, meager as it might be, which takes us to the topic of dowries—and that will take us to jolly old St. Nicholas.

> Whether through the kind of dowry that today's middle-class parents pass on in wedding gifts and home down payments, or the corporate mergers of medieval aristocratic families that might have taken years to negotiate, or the small businesses launched when two well-trained vintners join their complementary skills and marriage portions, marriage has always been a key way of organizing society's economy. Or to put it more bluntly: marriage is always about money.[1]

St. Nicholas was a fourth-century bishop in the part of the Mediterranean world now called Turkey. His symbol is three gold discs on a blue background. According to one of the most familiar stories about Nicholas, there was once a poor man who, like Tevye, had three daughters. The man was disconsolate because he could not provide a dowry for any of his daughters. Unable to support them or marry them off without a dowry, his only choice was to sell them into slavery or prostitution.

Bishop Nicholas heard about the man's plight and arranged to have three bags of gold thrown through the man's window. With dowries in hand, the daughters could now be married!

Dowries, such as Nicholas' bags of gold tossed through the window, travel from the bride's family to the groom or his father. Part of the reason for the dowry is to ensure that the bride will have some security (in some cases by getting the dowry back) if her husband dies or divorces her. In addition to this concern for justice, though, the size of a woman's dowry has historically had a direct relationship to her marriageability. "For richer, for poorer" may be the vow that is taken now, but it's clear where the emphasis has been placed when it comes to the topic of a dowry.

The tradition of dowries is complex and varied, but stories such as the three bags of money sailing through the window remind us that marriage has had a great deal to do with property and wealth. When someone is described as being a "good catch," one can assume that part of the goodness has to do with finances.

The opposite of a dowry is the "bride-price," which travels from the groom's family to the bride or her father. An example of this is found in a very matter-of-fact, but quite sobering, passage from the Mishnah, in which ancient Jewish law provided that "a daughter is . . . perceived as the property of her father; he collects the bride-price from the man who marries her or from one who seduces or rapes her (Exod. 22:16–17; Deut. 22:28–29) whether or not the violator marries her. The bride-price compensates for loss of the daughter's virginity, which is treated as the father's economic asset."[2] Not much question here about who owns what.

Whether it be Tevye and Lazer Wolf (who, as we hear in Yenta's song, "is a good man, a fine man, and well off!") negotiating a marriage contract or characters in a Jane Austen novel discussing the financial assets of a prospective spouse or the final scene in the movie *My Big Fat Greek Wedding* in which the newlyweds are shown in front of the house given to them by the bride's father, we have to be honest and unsentimental about making sure that our portrait of marriage is framed with little bags of gold and a lot of dollar signs. An awful lot of marriage arrangements involve who gets what stuff out of the deal.

A fascinating subtradition of arranged marriages were "morganatic marriages"—situations in which members of royal families in Europe contracted marriage with persons of inferior rank with the proviso that titles and property would not be passed on to the next generation. Can we see a modern parallel in prenuptial agreements in which very careful arrangements are made regarding who will own what in case a marriage fails? To pursue some of these situations in more detail would be another interesting side trip on our journey, but that would slow us down too much.

Families don't like to see hard-earned (or inherited) property disappear, especially to someone from outside their tribe or social class. Dowries and bride-price customs are just the tip of an economic iceberg that floats through the history of marriage. The joining together of a man and woman in marriage is much more than the creation of a new human relationship; it has been and continues to be the creation of a business partnership. And in any business deal, it's very common for each party to spell out exactly what the assets are and who gets what stuff. Not a very romantic tradition, but there it is.

RESISTANCE TO MIXED MARRIAGES

> The people of Israel, the priests and the Levites, have not separated themselves from the peoples of the lands with their abominations, from the Canaanites, the Hittites, the Perizzites, the Jebusites, the Ammonites, the Moabites, the Egyptians, and the Amorites. For they have taken some of their daughters as wives for themselves and for their sons. Thus the holy seed has mixed itself with the peoples of the lands. (Ezra 9:1–2)

Post-exile Israel: Get rid of foreign spouses!

One of the most amazing stories in all of human history is the persistence and perseverance of the Jewish people. Beginning as a ragtag group of nomads trekking around the ancient Near East, their patriarchs and matriarchs settled in the land of Canaan, then moved to Egypt, where they became enslaved. Guided by

God and led by Moses and Miriam and Aaron, the slaves escaped from slavery and returned to Canaan. They set up their tribal communities and were able to fight off the encroachment of the Philistines and other foreigners, but that necessitated the formation of a monarchy to unify and govern the country.

As various empires waxed and waned, the struggling nation on the eastern shore of the Mediterranean always had a "boot on its neck." In the eighth century B.C.E., the Assyrian Empire subjugated the Northern Kingdom of Israel; then, about 150 years later, the Babylonian Empire smashed the Southern Kingdom of Israel and took the political and religious leaders of Judah into exile. It was a profound crisis for the Jewish community. Would the people whose experience led them to believe that God had chosen them for a special mission in the world disappear from history? Would this heroic group that had survived for so many centuries as an intact community be assimilated into a foreign culture and lose its distinctive character? Would this holy people that sought to be a unique witness to communal justice and compassion be absorbed into the culture of "the peoples of the lands"?

Those questions become focused in a dramatic way in the sixth and fifth centuries B.C.E., during the exile in Babylon and the return to Judea. In Babylon, a "faithful remnant" of the Jewish people held onto their faith by maintaining customs that would bind the community together. By stressing Sabbath observance, circumcision, and special dietary practices, and also by undertaking a reinvigorated study of Torah, the people and their leaders were able to maintain their traditions and hold onto their unique identity.

However, when it came to marriage, there were problems. At this point, I don't see a new portrait to add to our collection so much as an impending crisis. During the two generations that the Jewish people resided in Babylon, many of the young people married outside the community. Instead of marriage within "our crowd," there were marriages with "their crowd." The elders in the community didn't like what was happening. That their young men were sowing their "holy seed" in foreign fields was to them an abomination. How can the community be kept holy and pure if the lineage is contaminated by foreign blood and the culture is diluted and maybe destroyed by foreign influences? With these concerns fueling their anxiety, the leaders took action when the Jews finally were allowed to return to the Holy Land.

The action they took could be symbolized by a picture of the severe priest, Ezra, standing before a group of married men and women in Jerusalem and pointing to the East as he proclaims, "We have broken faith with our God and have married foreign women from the peoples of the land, but even now there is hope for Israel in spite of this. So now let us make a covenant with our God to send away all these wives and their children . . . and let it be done according to the law" (Ezra 10:2–3).

Not a very heart-warming picture, is it? This is endogamy with a fierceness that is frightening. Ezra's proclamation shows us how inevitable it is for marriage to get deeply intertwined with both the law and with God. It is the expression on Ezra's face that we need to consider at this point, though. The determined look on his face, a combination of worry and anger, is the same expression that we can see on the faces of countless immigrant parents who see their children being assimilated into a strange culture. It's the same expression that we see on the face of the Amish patriarch in the movie *Witness*, when an outsider (played by Harrison Ford) comes into their tight-knit community, threatens their traditions with his "English" ways, and even cozies up to a beautiful young Amish widow (played by Kelly McGillis). As the Amish elder looks at what is happening to his daughter, his face becomes the face of Ezra and the face of any parent who is fearful of one of his or her children becoming involved in a "mixed marriage" with someone from "the outside."

And that takes us back to Tevye.

Tevye's third daughter

Tevye is a man of tradition. Even when he doesn't know the reason that a specific tradition exists, he still fiercely upholds that tradition. Why? "Because . . . it's tradition!"

During most of the Fiddler story, Tevye's basic compassion and his deep love for his daughters enables him to transcend the

Anatevka tradition of arranged marriages. He allows his first two daughters to enter marriages that were neither arranged by Yenta nor negotiated with the head of another family. Tevye breaks with tradition in order to achieve a higher good—in this case, the happiness and well-being of his daughters. In each case, he sings quietly to himself, "But look at my daughter's face, look at my daughter's eyes . . . she loves him . . ."

But such was not the case with his third daughter, Chava. She met and fell in love with Pietka, an outsider—a Russian, a Gentile, a Christian, a foreigner. In many ways, this young man was an enemy in Tevye's eyes. It was Pietka's people who carried out a mini-pogrom against the Jews of Anatevka. To make matters even worse, this horrible act of violence occurred on the night of Tzeitel's wedding. And now Chava has the temerity to want to marry this young man. Tevye replies in anger, "Don't forget who you are and who that man is. He's a different kind of man." Chava replies, "The world is changing, Papa." Tevye's anger rises even more as he shouts, "Some things will never change! Marrying outside the faith? No!"

Confronted by Golde, his wife, about what has happened, Tevye utters the heart-breaking words, "She is dead to us. We'll forget her." Finally, as Tevye and his family prepare to leave their village because they have been ordered out by the Russian authorities (Pietka's people!), Chava and Pietka make one last attempt to get her father's blessing. She agonizingly pleads, "I beg you to accept us." Tevye weighs the options—denying everything he believes in or denying his own daughter? Turning his back on his own faith and his own people or turning his back on his daughter? He concludes with the searing words, "If I bend, I'll break. NO!"

As Chava and Pietka walk away disconsolately, Tzeitel calls out, "Good-bye!" Then, in a brief moment of bending, Tevye says quietly, "And God be with you."

We cannot help feeling great sadness as we watch Tevye going in one direction and his third daughter in the other. Yet at the same time we understand that he is dealing with profound issues. How much can he bend? How far can he go outside the boundaries of the traditions he has honored all his life? How many times can he compromise and still maintain his integrity? What are his cherished beliefs worth if he easily casts them aside?

As Chava and Pietka disappear from view, we need to ask a different set of questions, such as: When do our traditions, especially our marriage traditions, close us off from new divine revelations and prevent us from going where the Spirit is trying to lead us? At what point does a tradition suffocate life instead of liberating us for new life? When does our narrow vision become like blinders so that we don't see the new portrait that is being painted right in front of us?

Those questions lead us inevitably to the historic tension between two racial groups in the United States.

Antimiscegenation in the United States

> Miscegenation (L. *miscere*, to mix, + *genus*, race) 1. An interbreeding of races. 2. Law. Intermarriage or interbreeding of whites and other races; used chiefly, in the U.S., of marriage with Negroes.[3]

I have visited Monticello twice. The first time was just at the time of the initial furor over the news about Thomas Jefferson's alleged intimate relationship with Sally Hemmings, a slave woman. We visited again many years later, and by that time, as a result of extensive research by historians and with the aid of DNA testing, most people who had looked carefully at the evidence had concluded that Jefferson had fathered several, if not all, of Sally Hemmings' seven children.

One of the many fascinating details in this story is that Sally Hemmings was actually the half-sister of Jefferson's wife, Martha, for John Wayles was Martha's father and also Sally Hemmings'. When Wayles died, Thomas and Martha inherited all of the Wayles' 135 slaves, including three-year-old Sally. A dozen years later, when Jefferson was sent to Paris to be the American minister to France, he had one of his daughters come to Paris to be with him (Jefferson's wife had died in 1782). Sally Hemmings accompanied Jefferson's daughter as a nursemaid. According to the records, when they all returned to the United States in 1789, Sally was pregnant.

This story is truly American. Though Jefferson was the genius of the American Revolution, he also incarnated the American paradox: ours is a country in which "all men are created equal," but, in good Orwellian fashion, some are more equal than others—and that meant especially white, propertied men who could increase their property (including slaves) by getting slave women pregnant. Even more ominously, if a white woman had sex with a black man, she became an outcast, along with any resulting children. And the black man who was involved was in danger of being lynched. But Thomas Jefferson and other plantation patriarchs could "mix their seed" outside "the tribe" in behavior that was more or less just the "good old boy" tradition. The late Senator Strom Thurmond, who fathered a biracial daughter, is a famous recent example of this tradition.

After slavery was abolished in the United States, there was great pressure to enforce racial boundaries through antimiscegenation laws, pressure that at one point in our history meant marriage between the races was barred in forty-one U.S. states and territories. The challenge for those who wanted to keep whites and Negroes from mixing was of course to define "Negro." In the nineteenth century, a person with one grandparent of African descent was deemed "black." But that changed.

> By the end of the nineteenth century and early in the twentieth, Southern states pushed the definition of "Negro" beyond the quadroon to one-eighth African heritage, then one-sixteenth (fifteen European great-grandparents and one African made you "black"), and finally, the infamous "one drop." In other words, people legally "white" in the nineteenth century became "black" in the twentieth—revealing as utter fiction any ideas about the races' fundamental difference. That one drop was taken quite literally, as if people could sift through corpuscles to find the contaminating "Negro" blood.[4]

The word that is especially tragic in the preceding excerpt is the word "contaminating." The horror with which some people react to miscegenation is based on what they perceive as contamination of something ("us," "our crowd," "our kind") that must be preserved at all costs. As they look at a white person with a "Negro" person (however that is defined), the one who sees this as contamination experiences antagonism, fear, and even hatred of "the other" or "the one from outside." This fear of contamination originates not in the head or the heart. It is a gut reaction that comes from deep within someone's identity. It can't be dealt with by rational arguments. It can only be altered through an experience that leads to some kind of "repentance" or change of heart. That is the work of prayer and the Spirit.

In our particular American history, racial tension has created an ongoing presence of either overt or covert "white supremacists." Equality be damned, they say. "We" are superior to "them." How sad it is to note the following situation: "At the end of the 1920s, forty-two states still banned marriage between whites and blacks, Mongolians, Hindus, Indians, Japanese, or Chinese. In the 1930s several states added 'Malays' to the list, a prohibition usually aimed at Filipinos."[5]

In *Fiddler on the Roof,* when the Russian Cossacks ride into the middle of the wedding celebration and destroy property and terrify the villagers, we see where this notion of "supremacy" can lead. There, anti-Semitism is fueling the violence. In the United States, racism is the culprit. In each case, someone is being rejected solely because of who they are—Jew, Gentile, black, foreigner, and so forth. And when that happens, there is a tragic resemblance among all the rejecters.

Sadly, we even have to look at Tevye's face when he shouts his loud "NO!" to his third daughter. Isn't his angry rejection of Chava and her new husband of a piece with the violent rejection that he and his people experience at the end of the story? It's a difference in degree—Tevye does not resort to violence—but not a difference in kind. Rejection is still rejection. But, fortunately, Tevye's final words to Chava, his heart-rending quiet blessing "And God be with you," offers some faint hope of a future reconciliation. One wishes she heard it.

ALTERNATIVES: JONAH AND RUTH

The author of the Book of Jonah could have written a very short book with the final verse saying, "You people's narrow-minded attitude makes me sick." Instead, the author chose to write a story that is more like a modern comic strip. The story of the wayward prophet Jonah is a very humorous little tale that pokes fun at the postexilic attempt to create a "pure" and exclusive community of faith. Jonah's refusal to have any dealings with the Gentiles up in Nineveh symbolizes the kind of actions that Ezra and Nehemiah took as they tried to rid their community of any contaminating influences. Their program included a demand for endogamous marriages. That narrow way of thinking makes the author of the Book of Jonah want to throw up—which is exactly what the big fish who swallowed Jonah does to Jonah.

At that point in the story, Jonah reluctantly trudges to Nineveh, half-heartedly preaches to the people there, and, lo and behold, they listen and repent! But not Jonah. He holds on to his self-righteousness and goes into a major sulk. As one writer has noted, this little book is about the "joy of hatred," which we see so clearly in Jonah's obnoxious behavior.

But instead of directly critiquing this kind of twisted joy, the author uses a far-fetched story full of irony and humor to open the readers' eyes to what is really going on when one people rejects another people. In that rejection, people are being much less gracious than the God who created all people, including "Nineveh, that great city, in which are more than a hundred and twenty thousand persons" (Jonah 4:11).

The Book of Jonah is only four chapters long. It is buried in the section of Hebrew Scriptures known as the "minor prophets," a designation given to them not because they are less important books, but just because they aren't very long.

The theme of Jonah, though, is not minor. It is about God's compassion and graciousness, with Jonah's nasty narrow mindedness as the dramatic foil. At the end of the book, the question arises: do I want to be like Jonah or do I want to see "the other" and "the outsider" as being acceptable to God and therefore to me? The answer to that question will go a long way toward helping people decide who is an appropriate person to marry. It is that question that we saw Tevye struggling mightily to answer.

Another book in Hebrew Scripture relates directly to this question. Like Jonah, the Book of Ruth is also only four chapters long, but in that beautiful story we find the same challenge to exclusivistic attitudes. At a time of famine in the land of Judah, Naomi and Elimelech and their two sons migrate to Moab, where the sons marry Moabite women, Orpah and Ruth. Tragedy strikes when first the father and then both sons die. All of that happens in the first five verses of the book.

The rest of the story is about the relationship between Naomi and Ruth and then the relationship between Ruth and Boaz. When Ruth decides to go back to Judah with Naomi, her mother-in-law, we hear the famous and poignant speech that begins, in the King James Version, with the words, "Intreat me not to leave thee or to return from following after thee . . ."

As the drama of these two remarkable women unfolds, Ruth the Moabite ends up marrying Boaz, a noble Jewish man. So much for endogamous marriage, right? Let's be sure to paint a picture of Boaz and Ruth on our canvas. It's a very dramatic contrast to the one preceding it, in which Ezra and the leaders of post-exilic Judaism forbid "intermarriage."

But the story doesn't just stop with this "exogamous" marriage. It makes an even more striking point when we discover that Ruth and Boaz produced a son, Obed, who became the father of Jesse. Then Jesse became the father of David, the one who began as a shepherd in the hills of Bethlehem and then rose to great fame and power as the greatest king in Jewish history. Not bad for someone who had a Moabite great-grandmother and whose blood therefore was not considered totally "pure."

The stories of Jonah and Ruth constitute a strong tradition within Hebrew Scripture. It is an alternative to the more narrow and exclusivistic attitude outlined in the previous section. Far from being a "minor" theme, it is a major counterbalance that tips the scales toward a more universalistic and compassionate viewpoint regarding "the other."

In the opening scene of *Fiddler on the Roof,* Tevye asks a rhetorical question, "How do we keep our balance?" His immediate answer is: "Tradition." In these two books of Jonah and Ruth, we find that a significant part of our tradition is in fact this move toward universalism, toward reaching out to "the other," toward accepting those whom we once called "enemy," and toward struggling deep in our heart to move toward reconciliation.

It is this universalism that is proclaimed in the third section of the Book of Isaiah, when the prophet declares that the Temple should be "a house of prayer for all peoples" (Isa. 56:7b), a phrase that Jesus uses when he makes his dramatic protest by briefly shutting down the Temple in Jerusalem as part of his own prophetic ministry. Now there's a real attention-getter. We will hear more from this man, Jesus, later in this book.

3

MARRIAGE FOR POLITICAL PURPOSES

We have looked at four major traditions of marriage so far in this book:

- Endogamous marriage (marriage "within the tribe"), exemplified by the marriage of Isaac and Rebekah
- Polygamous endogamy, exemplified by the marriage of Jacob and his two wives (and his two concubines)
- Levirate marriage (marriage to the brother-in-law)
- Arranged marriages

In exploring these traditions, we noted the dramatic strength of resistance to intermarriage, whether it be marriage outside the tribe or outside the racial group. Then, by noting the alternative tradition of a more universalistic approach to "foreigners" and "outsiders," and thereby to intermarriage, we saw that there are definitely two competing voices in our Judeo-Christian scriptural heritage. The first voice says, "Stay within our own crowd and our own tradition. Stay separate from other cultures and contaminating influences. Build up the holy community and keep it pure." The second voice says, "All people are included within God's creation. Be gracious to all people, as God is gracious. Accept those who are different from you and welcome strangers and outsiders."

The tension between these two perspectives is difficult to resolve. They both are strong traditions within Scripture and later became two different ways of being the church: the first led to a more exclusive and pure vision of the church, the second led to a more inclusive vision of the church. The symbol of the first might be walls, while the symbol of the second might be bridges. Those two visions are still with us in the church.

In general, our contemporary Western culture has moved beyond all four of the traditions outlined above. There may still be some of the same impulses to keep marriage within one's social, religious, or racial group, but for the most part, we no longer strictly observe any of the historic traditions that were so prominent in the early stages of our Judeo-Christian heritage.

What, then, were some of the ways in which the tradition of endogamy was overturned, especially for political purposes? We begin with King David and King Solomon.

"King Solomon loved many foreign women"

> "King Solomon loved many foreign women along with the daughter of Pharaoh: Moabite, Ammonite, Edomite, Sidonian, and Hittite women . . ." reads 1 Kings 11:1 in the revised standard version of the Bible. "He had seven hundred princesses and three hundred concubines and his wives turned away his heart." Add a pickup and it's a country song![6]

Solomon's father, King David, had quite an impressive marriage track record. Before becoming king, David took two wives. Then, when he moved to Jerusalem, he "took more concubines and wives" (2 Sam. 5:13). At that point, the real soap opera (or country western song?) began. David saw Bathsheba, the wife of Uriah the Hittite, and used his power to get rid of Uriah and take Bathsheba as his wife. Not a very heart-warming story in terms of

David's ethical rigor, but let's give the Hebrew historians credit for not whitewashing the story.

For our purposes, it is important to note that David had no compunction about wooing and marrying a "foreign" woman. Long gone were the days when a patriarch such as Abraham forbade his son to marry "the girl next door" because she was a Canaanite. David looked right next door, liked what he saw, and very soon Bathsheba the Hittite was his wife.

David and Bathsheba's son, Solomon, obviously inherited that propensity to marry whomever he wanted, in spite of the historic warning against intermarriage ("You shall not enter into marriage with them . . ." 1 Kings 11:2). That warning is an example of the first voice within Hebrew Scripture that upheld the tradition of "purity" in order to keep the community intact and holy. Solomon's marriages blasted that tradition right out of the water. With that in mind, though, it is difficult to see Solomon as an example of the more universalistic tradition. Solomon was clearly motivated by desires other than "purity," but it is hard to see his thousand wives/concubines as an example of the compassion and "inclusive tradition" exemplified by Boaz and Ruth. Indeed, in Solomon's case, no matter how much "love" and "heart" might have been involved, it seems best to see his marriages as primarily political.

Solomon was politically astute and learned quickly how a successful king carries out foreign policy:

> Solomon's foreign policy rested on securing political alliances and developing trade with the surrounding countries. As had always been the custom with monarchs, diplomatic relations were cemented with suitable marriages. Solomon was a notable exponent of this harem statecraft, and early in his reign he brought off a political coup of the first magnitude by marrying the daughter of the Egyptian Pharaoh.[7]

Following that marriage, Solomon seems to have had a dalliance with the Queen of Sheba and then began to build up his very large harem. To please his many wives and concubines,

Solomon gave them facilities for worshipping their own foreign gods. From the point of view of the faithful, the result of Solomon's behavior was tragic: "His wives turned away his heart after other gods; and his heart was not true to the Lord his God, as was the heart of his father David." (1 Kings 11:4) In this summary statement, we see that David gets good marks for his religious loyalty (although his ethics still left a lot to be desired), but Solomon was way out of line.

The key thing to note for this study is how unconstrained these two monarchs were by the tradition of endogamous marriage. Indeed, they exploited exogamy totally. The motive in these marriages, of course, was to forge political alliances. In later history, especially in Europe, this tradition of marriage for political purposes became very common. Marriages continued to be arranged, not by Yenta-style matchmakers, but by politically savvy monarchs and their advisors. Their concern was to use marriage to make political deals, to forge alliances, to preserve the peace, or to gain land—or at least reduce the risk of losing it.

Because this book is meant only as very brief exploration of the history of marriage, we will not go into any detailed sketch of the long history of intermarriage between various European royal families. Instead we will focus on just one example. It's a big jump chronologically from the portrait of Solomon and his huge harem directly to King Henry VIII in sixteenth-century England, but in terms of marriage, those two monarchs have a lot in common.

"I'm Henry the Eighth, I am . . ."

Henry VII of England arranged for his son, Arthur, to be married to Catherine of Aragon because an alliance with Spain would enable him to dominate France, the ancient enemy. When Arthur died before his father, it seemed logical to pass Catherine on to Arthur's younger brother. The fact that church law forbade a woman to marry her deceased husband's brother seemed far less important to the English king, the Spanish emperor, and the Roman pope than the political advantages to be gained.[8]

In the preceding quotation, we immediately notice that the tradition of levirate marriage has been rejected in most cases. Had it still been in effect, the marriage of young Henry and Catherine of Aragon would have been readily accepted. But the civil and religious laws of sixteenth-century England were a long way from ancient Israel's laws, especially with regard to marriage. Yet the tradition of arranged marriages was still firmly established.

In the enormously complex story of Henry VIII and his marriages, we see above all that politics played a central role. As in King Solomon's day, marriage was used to cement political alliances. But there was one crucial difference between those two monarchies: Henry VIII ruled at a time when monogamy was the requirement in marriage and the church had evolved a huge compendium of laws that controlled monogamous marriage.

And there's the rub for Henry VIII. Not permitted the wildly polygamous marriages that abounded in ancient Israel, Henry was in a real pinch. Not only was he very worried that there were no male heirs from his marriage to Catherine, there was also the matter of Anne Boleyn. But, as we know, the Catherine of Aragon/Anne Boleyn situation was only the beginning of Henry's gruesome soap opera.

Historians and theologians are appropriately careful to note that Henry VIII did not "found a new church." The history of the Anglican Church is very complex and had developed its own identity over many centuries before it finally repudiated papal authority during the reign of Henry VIII. Henry's marital situation certainly brought things to a head, as it were, and makes for some very spicy reading. But for our purposes, it is important to note that as recently as the sixteenth century, political maneuvering was at the heart of marriage arrangements, at least at the royal level.

4

MARRIAGE FOR PROCREATION

"In the introduction to the marriage rite for the first Book of Common Prayer (1549), Thomas Cranmer presented three purposes for marriage: for procreation, as a remedy for sexual frustration, and for companionship."[9]

For most of human history, men and women have coupled in order to produce babies and ensure the survival of the tribe or clan or family. When plague or famine or disease or even childbirth itself decimated ancient populations, it was necessary to procreate so that there would be a next generation.

The context for the famous command in Genesis to "be fruitful and multiply" (Gen. 1:28) most likely originated in the experience of the exilic and postexilic Jewish community. At that time, there was great concern that assimilation, dwindling of the population, and the fragility of human life in the ancient world threatened the very existence of the Jewish people. So the obvious solution was to have more babies in order to ensure the survival of the community. In that situation, it is not surprising to find a command to procreate.

But humans also reproduced to increase the labor supply. In our modern, affluent American culture, in which most children are valued for their unique identities, not for what they can contribute to the economic well-being of the family, it is hard for us to understand how the basic family unit has radically changed from what it used to be for many centuries. Formerly, children, along with slaves and servants, were needed to get work done. Caring for the animals, gathering firewood, fetching water from the well, washing clothes in the river, grinding grain, picking berries, taking goods to market—the list of chores went on and on. So, naturally, the more people available to do this work, the better life would be, and the most natural way to get more people was to make babies.

In recent times in America, there has been a great effort by political and social leaders to convince young couples to delay sexual intercourse until after marriage. This is a very different tradition from that of some of our ancestors. In sixteenth-century England, when Thomas Cranmer wrote the first Book of Common Prayer, in which he listed the primary purpose of marriage as being the procreation of children, one out of every three first babies was conceived before—not after—the wedding. In 1800, in postcolonial North America, the number of women whose first children were born soon after marriage was also one in three. This was often seen as the "traditional" way. If marriage is primarily for making babies, then let's get started on that project right away and not wait for a wedding!

I had never heard of a "trothplight baby" until I began doing research for this book. That interesting term was used to describe a baby who was born after betrothal but before the wedding. It apparently was not a pejorative term. It just described the reality of a couple who were doing what their culture desired them to do—increase the population. For much of our history, fruitfulness was more important than wedding ceremonies, and in some places, the marriage might even be called off if the bride were not pregnant!

Another word I had not encountered before doing this research is "handfasting"—which described some medieval betrothals. It was a solemn and binding covenant that was basically equivalent to marriage and was sometimes consummated immediately after a betrothal ceremony. Therefore, to have a pregnant bride at a wedding might be called "traditional" for some eras.

I can't help but wonder if, at the time of these "handfasted" relationships that often produced "trothplight" children, there was what we might call a "reverse shotgun wedding"? ("You'd better be pregnant or we're in big trouble!") That sounds very strange to us, yet the fact that I can even make that suggestion indicates how times have changed—and marriage with it.

The idea of a "trothplight" baby is more than an idiosyncratic detail in this particular portrait of marriage. Consider the following verse: "Now the birth of Jesus the Messiah took place in this way. When his mother Mary had been engaged to Joseph, but before they lived together, she was found to be with child from the Holy Spirit" (Matt. 1:18). As a Christian, I need to acknowledge that the key person in my spiritual history, Jesus, was none other than a "trothplight" baby! (And now I can look forward to a new translation of Matthew that will describe Mary and Joseph as being "handfasted"!)

Part of our task in this book about marriage is to see where we have been in the past, where we might be headed in the future, and how God has been intimately involved in this long and fascinating history. Whatever one thinks about the doctrine of the virgin birth, we probably all agree that there can't be a more intimate involvement of God with a human couple than Mary's pregnancy—which occurred, according to Matthew and Luke, outside what we would call "the institution of marriage." In the case of any "trothplight" baby, instead of procreation being a purpose of marriage, it was actually almost more important than marriage.

But the situation has changed. In a world that is already overpopulated, many people are thinking a great deal about how procreation fits into marriage and into the world of the future. In developing countries of the southern hemisphere, the need for large families to ensure the survival and "social security" of the family may still be more of a reality than in the developed countries of the northern hemisphere. In North America, which has only about 6 percent of the world's population, can we continue on a course in which we consume an enormously disproportionate percentage of the earth's resources and generate an equally disproportionate amount of the world's refuse and pollution?

With the rise of industrialization and the development of our modern economic systems, it is not surprising that a major reordering of priorities for marriage has occurred in recent centuries. Instead of children being a necessity, they are much more a matter of choice. As a result, procreation has become less important as a purpose for marriage.

So even with a continuing strong and natural desire for more babies to be born, the tradition of procreation being central to marriage has definitely and, in view of a burgeoning world population, necessarily, been weakened. As we look at a marriage portrait with many children in the spotlight, can we accept the fact that succeeding generations, succeeding layers of this portrait, may have a very different interpretation of how many children there should be in the picture?

✵ 5 ✵

FOUR REVOLUTIONARY MARRIAGE TRADITIONS FROM THE CHURCH

"The early Yahwistic community was committed to the equality of its members, and indeed we can recognize a persistent egalitarian impulse influencing the laws and institutions of early Israel. . . . The social and ethical legacy of early Yahwism is one of the most remarkable in history."[10]

Taking our Judeo-Christian heritage seriously, we recall that our spiritual ancestors were slaves and that the original good news, or gospel, was about the God who "brought you out of the land of Egypt, out of the house of slavery" (Exod. 20:2). From that dramatic revelation of a God who is on the side of the poor and oppressed, we can go straight to the Christian proclamation about Christ Jesus, "who, though he was in the form of God, did not regard equality with God as something to be exploited, but emptied himself, taking the form of a slave" (Phil. 2:6–7).

In the Jewish and Christian communities at their best, there is no room for hierarchy or domination. The God who formed these communities reveals an amazing egalitarian impulse in the divine way of acting, with the inevitable result that the communities should be governed by that same impulse. This expectation and reality is captured most dramatically in St. Paul's affirmation: "There is no longer Jew or Greek, there is no longer slave or free, there is no longer male and female; for all of you are one in Christ Jesus" (Gal. 3:28).

SLAVES AND CITIZENS CAN MARRY

This radical call for equality had implications for marriage, particularly when it came to slaves. In the Roman Empire, persons of one social class were not permitted to marry someone from a different class and it certainly was unacceptable for a citizen to marry a slave. Under Roman law, slaves were not even allowed to marry each other. This tradition was mirrored in the United States when slaves were not able to enter into legal marriages and therefore established their own customs such as "jumping the broom" to make a public declaration of their marriages.

Yet, "from the beginning, the church was willing to break the law by allowing slaves and freedmen to marry citizens."[11] Here is a revolutionary development in the history of marriage. These early Christians took seriously the example of Jesus, who steadfastly resisted separating people into class categories, and took seriously Paul's insistence on the inherent equality of people who are "in Christ." Even though the marriages between "slave and free" had to travel under the radar of the Empire, the church was being faithful to a radical idea that will always challenge any attempt to keep marriage within the boundaries of class or race or any other arbitrary designation.

What a fascinating new portrait to add to our collection! Maybe it could be in the form of a mosaic, like the ones found on the floors and walls of ancient churches. The fading portrait would show one person dressed in the garb of a citizen and the other person dressed in slave's clothing. But the two people would be holding hands with each other while a shadowy divine hand of blessing hovers over them. Non-Christians of that time would have shuddered to see that couple, but this kind of relationship that transcends class distinctions is a solid part of our tradition of marriage.

The old hymn proclaims, "In Christ there is no east or west, in him no north or south, but one great fellowship. . . ."[12] Breaking down human barriers has always been a central aspect of spreading the good news, so the early Christians' permitting marriage between slave and free was their first revolt against the culture in which they lived. The second revolt was even more dramatic and much stranger.

CELIBACY

The early Christians' rejection of marriage was a jaw-dropping event. Going against the tide of centuries of tradition and rebelling against the Hebrew culture from which it grew, the early church took the unusual position that it is not necessary to marry in order to be an authentic human being; in some cases, as Paul advised in 1 Corinthians 7:38, it might even be better if one does not marry.

This was a very strange rebellion, but there it is, recorded in history and lived out by many Christians over the past two millennia. In the early Christian experience, based as it was on the belief in resurrection and the passing away of this world, people were not primarily concerned about the continuation of any family or tribe. They were part of a new creation that transcended history and culture and they were therefore independent of an institution such as marriage. If one is a disciple of Jesus, who according to the received record was not married, and if one believes that one's identity is ultimately found in the transhistorical realm of God, why then get married?

Yet this rejection of marriage, revolutionary as it was, was also intertwined with a very ambivalent attitude toward that key aspect of marriage: sex. On the one hand, early Christians had inherited from their Jewish ancestors the belief that creation and human embodiment are good, but at the same time, the early Christian theologians and church leaders were extremely suspicious of any activity that was too pleasurable or that would woo believers away from their essential spiritual destinies. One way to resolve that tension was to simply refrain from marriage and sex altogether, which is what led some Christians to live celibate lives and to believe that virginity brings one closer to God.

As these revolutionary ideas became embedded in the church, even those who did marry were deeply influenced by this new understanding. Western Christianity was especially affected by the life and writings of St. Augustine, who struggled mightily to rise above his own sensual past. The result was that for many married couples, sexual intercourse became sort of a necessary evil that was engaged in solely for procreation and certainly not for pleasure.

> The monks and theologians offered a little jump-start toward angelic life by helpfully ruling sex off-bounds just as often as they could—for instance, during menstruation, pregnancy, or nursing (which could be as long as two years), and on holy days—such as Thursdays, in memory of Jesus' betrayal, Fridays, in memory of his death, Saturdays, in honor of the Virgin Mary, on Sundays, of course, on Mondays, in memory of the departed souls, as well as forty days before Easter, Pentecost, Christmas, on feasts, fasts, and even—imagine!—on the wedding night and a few days after, to train you for a lifetime of continence."[13]

This probably strikes us as a fairly strange world in which to live—and one has to wonder how many Christians actually followed the regimen prescribed above—but the fact that this vision of sexuality was being proclaimed meant that the portrait of marriage was being changed radically. If nonpleasurable sex was the rule within marriage, then, of course it would be better to not even get entangled in such a troublesome activity. So virgins and celibates move to the center of the stage.

As we contemplate those celibate monks and nuns and priests and countless single people who have chosen to live a celibate life in order to be faithful to their particular vocations, we should, I think, resist our own hypersexualized culture's tendency to view these celibates as extraordinarily weird and somehow less than fully human.

For example, I recently had the opportunity during a retreat at an Episcopal monastery to eat lunch and converse with one of the life-professed monks. To hear his moving explanation of what he has experienced as "the gift of celibacy" helps to put to rest the stereotype that a life of celibacy is a disordered life of sexual repression. The monk spoke eloquently about how his commitment to a life of celibacy enabled him to be available to a much wider range of people, within the monastery and among people who came to the monastery as retreatants, to whom he could offer his ministry of counseling and spiritual companionship because it is clearly unencumbered by any sexual implications. This particular monk seems to me to be an excellent example of one way that a person can be authentically human and faithfully Christian without being married. The genuine joy exuding from this monk is a dramatic reminder that some people who are called to the single life can be enormously helpful to many people, including weary clergy who come to a retreat house looking for refreshment, homeless teenagers who are welcomed into a house of refuge where they can be safe for at least a little while, or "seekers" who are looking for an experience of holiness that they cannot find in ordinary communities and relationships.

I was reared in a family in which my father died when I was four years old and my mother never remarried. Did she ever make a conscious choice after her husband's death to live a celibate life? I don't know. Did she simply never meet anyone who could measure up to what she had experienced with my father? Possibly. Was she viewed by people in our town in the 1950s Midwest as being a bit odd because she "didn't have a man?" Probably. Yet her life of single parenthood had something in common with that monk's experience of the gift of celibacy. My mother did not make the same kind of choice as the monk and the monk didn't have two biological children as dependents, but there is still a connection between their lives and they both are definitely rooted in the ancient revolutionary tradition initiated by the church and lived out by thousands—millions?—of

Christians who choose not to marry and who can teach us all much about living a healthy and holy life in community and in solitude.

Our jaws may still drop a bit as we look at those single-minded celibates standing in front of our portrait of marriage, but we cannot linger too long here because we have to move to the next revolutionary tradition, which has always encountered a great deal of resistance and continues to do so in the twenty-first century—the tradition that women are equal to men.

WOMEN ARE EQUAL TO MEN

According to the first chapter of Genesis, God created humankind as male and female, equal partners as they mirror the being of God, which is a mysterious blend of community and unity. Humans are made in that divine image, so any kind of hierarchy and domination, especially if it is based on gender, would be excluded from the divine plan.

But then we turn the page and encounter the story of Adam and Eve in Genesis 2. Without pausing for much of a breath, we suddenly are tempted to think that female subordination is part of the created order. I mean, after all, there it is right there in the story—Eve was made after Adam and therefore Adam is superior, right?

A closer reading of the story suggests that the story is not as clear and unambiguous as some may wish. If we really want to search the story about Adam and Eve for its teaching on the equality—or inequality—of human males and females, we have three choices:

- We can say that Adam was formed first; therefore, males are preeminent. This has been a very popular interpretation for millennia and one does not have to be an astute historian or sociologist or theologian to know how deeply the tradition and customs of patriarchy are imbedded in our Judeo-Christian culture.
- We can say that Eve was formed last and therefore she was meant to rule. "Save the best 'til last" is the motto here.

After all, the story itself tells us that Adam was formed from dust but Eve was formed from human flesh and bone, which means we could say she is made of much better material! As one commentator has written good-humoredly: Eve is the Adam upgrade, version 2.0 of man.[14]

- Instead of either of these choices, we can resist the temptation to enlist Adam and Eve in the ongoing debate about the equality of women and men and just let the story invite us to see how relationship and community are at the heart of God and therefore are the essence of what it means to be made in God's image. And in a truly human community, as in the heart of God, domination is not part of the picture.

As briefly described in chapter 1, I have in this book made the third choice and want to be honest about that point of view. But I am mindful of the cacophony of voices that want to make strong claims for either the first or the second choice. Those two points of view clash throughout Scripture, although the patriarchal voice of the first choice seems to be especially loud and has had enormous influence in the Jewish and Christian communities for many centuries.

In such a brief history of marriage, it is absolutely impossible to review all the ups and downs of the vision of human equality that seems to be rooted in the first chapter of Genesis and is enshrined in the second chapter of Paul's letter to the Galatians. Even the few books listed in the bibliography that deal with this issue are just the tip of an enormous iceberg of literature, scholarship, and political writing that has been accumulating for centuries. It would be incredibly presumptuous to think that anyone, including me, could present a fair summary of all the ideas and positions about gender equality (or inequality) that have been put forth for thousands of years by poets, prophets, pundits, and preachers.

For our purposes suffice it to state that I am persuaded by prayer, reflection, and experience to say that the principle of gender equality is at the heart of Scripture and Christian faith. I am mindful of the way that some parts of Scripture have been used to buttress the case for the preeminence of male over female, and sometimes vice versa, but as I look at Jesus and see how he conducted himself with women, I celebrate the fact that he was not constrained by inherited notions of male superiority and that he nurtured the seeds that ultimately grew into the revolutionary tradition in which women and men are treated as wholly equal.

This tradition of equality has not fared very well in the church or in society, and certainly has not been the hallmark in many marriages, but if we are painting an honest portrait of marriage as intended by the Creator instead of marriage as lived out by many human couples, we would need to paint a picture in which neither partner dominates and both partners find equal authenticity and meaning in their avowed vocation of marriage.

And that takes us back to that lunch table at the monastery. When the monk spoke of "the gift of celibacy," besides helping me understand his experience of not being married, was he also inviting me to reflect on "the gift of marriage" that I have been given? Is that the best context in which this discussion of gender equality can occur? If we begin with an acknowledgment that a holy and healthy marriage is founded on the grace of God and a couple's grateful response to the gift they have been given, can we make some headway towards creating a partnership of equality and love between two people?

The answer to that question may not be an immediate "Yes" from everyone, but we must wrestle with that question in order to consider the fourth revolutionary marriage tradition initiated by the church: that of lifelong commitment.

LIFELONG COMMITMENT

Today there is much hand wringing over the frequency of divorce. It is a very common occurrence to hear the lament that "half of our marriages end in divorce." But before we begin exploring this lament's background—which is the radical vision of the church that marriages should be lifelong—we should be historically honest and celebrate the fact that the average marriage today lasts longer than those of the past. For example, in early nineteenth-century England, about one-third of marriages were ended by death within fifteen years. In France at that same time, the marriages of peasants lasted an average of twelve to seventeen years.[15]

The key reality of marriage for most of our history has been that one of the partners, usually the woman, died at an early age. If one's life expectancy is only thirty or forty years, it is much less of a dramatic commitment to say that one will be married "'til death do us part" than to make that same vow when there is a fairly good chance that both partners will live into their seventies or eighties. So, even with the frequency of divorce in modern society, in general, we are still staying married for a longer time on average than did our ancestors. Our forebears had low divorce rates but high death rates. We have been able, through economic progress and the advances of modern medicine and nutrition, to achieve exactly the opposite: high divorce rates and low premature death rates.

This brief celebration of the relative longevity of modern marriages is one way to begin describing the revolutionary tradition of lifelong commitment. In no way have we achieved the goal of all couples remaining bound to each other until they are parted by death, but our disappointment over the frequency of divorce is at least testimony to the idea that things were not meant to be this way.

The early church began in a culture in which divorce was quite common. In both Jewish and Roman culture, divorce was fairly easy to accomplish and was usually initiated by the man. Las Vegas "quickie" divorces were still far in the future, but some of the same reality still prevailed. Get a few witnesses to hear your complaint and jump through a few legal hoops, and you were divorced—usually to the significant economic and social detriment of the woman.

The early Christians had a different vision. Partly out of the same respect for women that they saw modeled by Jesus, who saw that women were most often treated unjustly by divorce procedures, and partly because Christians envisioned themselves to some degree as a "new creation" set apart from the society around them, Christians took seriously Jesus' teaching that divorce was basically not permitted. There are volumes and volumes of commentary and legal interpretations about what Jesus' teaching "really" means for us today, but the early Christians recognized that they were being called to live differently than those around them. And that meant if you marry, you are making a lifetime commitment. One wife, one husband, and no fooling around. As incredible as that custom was in a very promiscuous society in the first century, so it is incredible now in what is possibly an even more promiscuous society.

The focus here is not on a comparison of marriages of the past with modern marriages and not a comparison of the relative promiscuity of ancient and modern society, but rather to hold up for a brief inspection this new feature added to the evolving portrait of marriage—the fact that in the Christian tradition there was the revolutionary development that marriage would be lifelong. We might depict this as a sequence of portraits, each of which features the same two people depicted as they age.

That sequence conflicts dramatically with what many modern couples experience, which is a series of two or more marriages with different partners. "Serial monogamy" is the catchphrase for this reality, but, again, this new reality is only possible because men and women are living much longer than they used to and therefore have much more time to see one or more of their marriages be parted by death—not always the death of a spouse, but the death of the marriage itself.

So, if you want to see some real jaw dropping, imagine how a premodern couple would react if they could open a local newspaper in the United States today and read without much fanfare about a local celebration to honor a couple who have been married for sixty or seventy years. An article in my local newspaper recently featured a 102-year-old man and a 100-year-old woman who had been married for eighty-three years! Many of our ancestors would probably be rendered speechless by even considering what it would be like to live to be eighty-three years old, so think what a shock it would be for them to think of being married to the same person for that many years. Quite a revolution!

A BRIEF SUMMARY

In this section of the book, I have quickly tried to describe four revolutionary marriage traditions initiated by the church: 1) permitting slaves and citizens to marry each other, 2) honoring celibacy as an authentic option for faithful Christians, 3) envisioning female and male equality, and 4) expecting marriage to be a lifelong commitment.

In each of these areas, the church as an institution and Christians as individuals and couples have often failed to live up to these visions or to hold fast to these traditions. Social class is still a powerful determinant of who marries whom. People who choose to live as singles are all too often seen as being somewhat abnormal (even the unfortunate use of the phrase "unmarried" to describe a single person implies that something is missing). The struggle for women's equality, even in the allegedly progressive West, continues. And many people are not able to follow through on the vow of lifelong commitment.

The fact that there is a less than stellar track record for Christians in adhering to these four traditions does not diminish the validity of the revolutionary ideals. It just means that living as a revolutionary is very hard work, has no guarantee of success, and depends a great deal on the grace and mercy of God and the willingness of singles and partners to live in the power of the Spirit.

6

WHAT MAKES A MARRIAGE VALID?

MUTUAL CONSENT

Mary and Joe had been courting for about a year. Their families approved of their relationship and most people who knew them fully expected them to marry. One beautiful Saturday night, with a light breeze moving through the warm summer air and with a full moon casting its glow on the path where they often went walking together, Joe and Mary felt especially close to each other as they ambled hand in hand toward the old apple orchard.

At the edge of the orchard, at the place where they often would stop and kiss, Joe suddenly turned toward Mary, put his hands on her shoulders, and said, "Mary, let's get married." Mary had been waiting for those words for a long time, but had not wanted to hurry Joe into a decision. She looked into his eyes, which were unusually wide open. Although it might have just been the luster from the moon, it did seem that Joe's eyes were startlingly bright and alive. He was both eager and nervous, but also focused on Mary in a way she had never seen before. With a surge of intense joy, Mary said, "Oh, yes, Joe, let's do!"

The key aspect of this portrait is that it shows two people consenting to marriage. And, for much of our history, no matter how dramatic or undramatic, romantic or unromantic the scene might be, this mutual consent has been all that is necessary for them to, indeed, *be* married.

The striking thing in this portrait is that Joe and Mary are the only people in it. There are no witnesses, no parents, no civil authorities, and no church officials. It is just the two of them, looking into each other's eyes and binding themselves together. In that moment, as their intentions are made known to each other and as they commit themselves to each other, they basically are married.

Of course, the portrait will be embellished once they get back to their homes and tell their family and friends and begin making plans for some kind of ceremony, but what happened out there on the edge of the apple orchard is at the heart of a tradition deeply imbedded in our Judeo-Christian history—the tradition that it is the mutual consent of the couple that validates the marriage.

Many people, especially concerned parents, dedicated civic and religious leaders, and upholders of "family values," get very nervous about this tradition. They have good cause to do so. Change just a few details in the scene—such as putting Joe and Mary on a blanket on a secluded beach with a couple of empty six-packs of beer next to them or putting the couple in the hayloft of a barn, with their clothes mostly off instead of on—and we can easily wonder if these two are making a mature and rational decision. In the latter two examples, one can appropriately raise questions about what part of the body is making the crucial response in this dramatic moment.

However, if we are being honest about the history of marriage, we have to accept that at the moment of mutual consent, regardless of whether the moon is full or the trees are apple or the clothes are mostly off, these two people have been seen as essentially married. Joe might as well take a piece of angel cake out of his backpack and offer it to Mary under that tree, because their munching on that soft cake is as symbolic of their union as any rings they might exchange or fancy wedding cake they will eat or documents they might later sign.

As we look at the portrait of Joe and Mary making their private vows to each other, most of us quickly want to add more details to the scene. We want there to be family members, especially parents and siblings who approve of this match. We want to be sure that the couple's good friends are there to support them as they pledge their troth to each other. And, presiding over the scene, we want some kind of authority—either civil or religious and preferably both at the same time if we live in a country or state in which clergy are licensed as officers of the state for purposes of saying that a couple is married. But, if we shrug off our inherited beliefs about marriage and focus on the essence of getting married, we have to leave all those other people out of the portrait. They are just icing on a cake: it is two people who make the marriage by agreeing to be married.

If, walking home from the orchard, Joe and Mary regard each other as spouses and behave accordingly, then, in actuality they are married. This tradition has great support in ancient Roman law and in long-standing Jewish custom. Indeed, as we will see in subsequent chapters, for the major part of church history, Christians needed no civil permission to marry and did not come to the church for a wedding.

The startling thing about this tradition is that, much to the chagrin of parents and moralists and respectable citizens, the modern trend of people living together "without benefit of clergy" or without a marriage license is actually just a reversion to the much more "normal" and "traditional" way of becoming married by mutual consent. And it's not just the young and starry-eyed who are doing this. Just ask at the retirement home down the street to find out which widows and widowers have taken to "being together" in a way that is not very dissimilar to what Joe and Mary began out there in the moonlight.

It is not unusual at my house, when the telephone rings, for me to pick it up and hear someone say, "Will you marry us?" I am usually polite when I reply that I will need to meet with the couple and talk with them for a while about why they want a priest to be involved in their wedding and what makes their relationship tick and how they view their future of being together in sickness and in health. But maybe the next time I get one of these calls, I will just say, "Have you two ever been out walking in the moonlight near an apple orchard? If so, what did you say to each other?" And, then, if they make the right answer, I can simply say, "Hey, you're basically already married, because in your own imperfect way you have made a mutual consent to each other... and if you are already living together and making love to each other (which is usually the case these days), you have consummated your relationship. Consent and consummation: sounds like marriage to me and to our tradition, so everything that happens from now on is just about formalizing things a bit."

Lest anyone think that I tried to sneak the consummation of marriage in there, let us leave that caller speechless on the other end of the telephone line and get on with a fuller consideration of what is the natural next step after mutual consent.

CONSUMMATION

On account of some people's discomfort, we have to leave the next canvas blank, or at least keep a curtain over it so that only those who choose to can actually look at it—because this canvas has sex as its central feature. Our portrait for this tradition of marriage should show the couple engaging in sexual intercourse.

Common sense suggests that marriage normally involves coitus, if for no other reason than the necessity of "doing it" in order to procreate, but the church has struggled mightily to incorporate healthy sexuality into its view of marriage.

Whether or not we make a graphic portrait of this aspect of marriage, we have to admit that Christians have had an extremely ambivalent attitude toward sexual intercourse as an essential part of marriage. The question to wrestle with here is: Is consummation necessary to validate a marriage? The natural answer for most people would be, "Well, of course." And, to be blunt, for many people at the beginning of their marriage, that's what it is all about. It is this answer, enshrined in pithy quips about "marriage making it legal" and innumerable jokes about what happens on various couple's wedding nights, that suggests that our portrait of marriage should show the couple bedded down together as indisputable proof that they are, indeed, married.

There are many fascinating customs in a variety of cultures that are emblematic of the fact that the act of having sex was central to marriage. At some ancient marriage celebrations, guests trooped from the wedding ceremony to the reception and then to the bedroom, so that they could be witnesses not just to the "plighting of the troth," but also to the sexual intercourse that was an essential part of the deal. The darker side of this voyeurism is seen in the imperative for there to be proof of the bride's virginity on that wedding night, since that often might have been part of the deal between the groom's family and the bride's family.

In spite of the modern tendency to make sexual intercourse a much more casual endeavor, for centuries it has been the tradition that marriage and sexual congress are infinitely intertwined and inextricably bound together. But many in the church, especially some of the fathers of the ancient church, did not sit very comfortably with this reality. St. Augustine, in trying to understand the presence of God in human relationships, including his own past relationships with his mistresses, was tormented by his conviction that marriage was good but sex was not. This was a real dilemma for Augustine, and the Western church's traditions of marriage have been deeply affected by Augustine's wrestling with marriage and sex.

Throughout its history, the church has had to wrestle with two key biblical stories that impinge on the tradition of consummation as a validating aspect of marriage. The first story is that of Adam and Eve. "The ancient rabbis usually maintained that Adam and Eve had consummated their marriage in the Garden of Eden. Some Jewish sources assumed that consummation had taken place outside the Garden."[16] When Christian writers began interpreting that story, squeamish as they were about sexual intercourse, many of them wanted to move the sex part of the Adam and Eve story as far away from paradise as possible and tie it up with the fall instead of with the goodness of creation.

But you already know that my own preference is to keep Adam and Eve far away from marriage, not from sex. I easily can imagine them "doing it" lustily and with great joy. "Tov meov, Adam! Very good. And how was it for you?" "Tov meov for me too, Eve. This really is a garden of delight. And how about if the two of us now go for a stroll in the cool of the evening?" In this interpretation, the primal couple savors the joy of creation in a most natural way and it is only later, down in Eden's orchard, that they get off course and bend the creation away from what the Creator had intended.

The second biblical story that must be wrestled with in terms of the consummation of a real marriage is the one that has made biblical interpreters scratch their heads furiously and show off their dancing skills as they sashay in and out of the story of Jesus' parents, Joseph and Mary. According to the story, this Joe and Mary were betrothed, which means there was in place a consent for them to marry. But, as we hear every year when we celebrate the nativity, "before they lived together, she was found to be with child from the Holy Spirit" (Matt. 1:18b). In Luke's telling of the story, the author records Mary as asking, "How can this be, since I am a virgin?" (Luke 1:34).

If we can possibly step back from the story of the nativity (and that may be very difficult for many people since the story is so deeply imbedded in our customs and our psyches), we can see that Matthew and Luke have given Augustine the perfect gift: a story in which a sexless marriage produces the most holy child ever born. For Augustine and his followers, it doesn't get much better. Procreation without all the messy details. Nice.

But in terms of marriage, we have a quandary here. If consummation is at the heart of marriage, then Joseph and Mary were not truly married. On the other hand, if consummation is not at the heart of marriage, an awful lot of people have made some wrong assumptions about the relationship of marriage and sexuality.

A third choice with regard to Jesus' parents, and one which I find actually very appealing, is to consider the possibility that within the customs of first-century Judaism, in which sexual intercourse was not an unusual aspect of betrothal, it is not inconceivable for Joseph and Mary to have mirrored Adam and Eve in a bit of sexual expression as part of their being betrothed. But such a portrait may not be one some people can consider.

The intent here is simply to raise the issue of whether we should paint our traditional married couple making love and thereby adhere to a strong tradition that sexual intercourse is inherently a part of marriage. Or, should we say that consummation is not a validating aspect of marriage and thereby allow plenty of room in our portrait for Jesus' parents as portrayed by Matthew and Luke and for countless other couples who have chosen to live their lives together in a variety of nonsexual ways?

These questions return us to the underlying question: what makes a marriage valid. And who should do the validating?

VALIDATION BY AN OUTSIDE AUTHORITY

What if the aforementioned Joe-of-the-Apple-Orchard is actually the oldest son of the Duke of Winchester, who has already arranged for Joe to marry the lovely Samantha, whose father is the lord of the adjoining manor? The duke will not be happy about Joe's little foray down the moonlit path with Mary.

Or, what if Mary is the only daughter of Colonel Ashley Jones, a distinguished officer in the Confederate Army and longtime plantation owner, but Joe is the son of the local blacksmith and is not known for being a hard worker? Or, even worse, what if Joe is not just a blacksmith, but is also black?

Or, what if Joe is from a long line of New Hampshire farmers and maple sugarers, but Mary, who just recently moved to town, is clearly a "flatlander" from New Jersey?

Whatever the details are in these particular portraits, or the infinite number of variations on the theme of "mutual consent" that could be painted, the powers that be, especially the parents, will be very nervous about Joe and Mary's situation. If it is the young couple's words and intentions that validate the marriage, well, it's just too . . . too chaotic . . . and they don't really know what they are doing . . . and what about the property that was supposed to be passed to Joe and Samantha, not Joe and Mary? . . . and, really, I mean . . . a blacksmith! . . . and why didn't we keep more control over who our child was spending time with . . . and . . .

In this ancient but still modern situation of impending marital chaos, many people want someone to assert control. An independent authority needs to decide who can marry whom and when they can marry and how they can marry and who inherits what and other such issues that are far removed from the scene in the apple orchard but are soon in the center of the picture. But who is going to settle all these disputes and calm down the parents and get these crazy kids straightened out?

In our history, there have been two authorities who have been given the responsibility for presiding over or controlling or blessing or certifying or doing something to keep marriage from just being validated in a magic moment in the moonlight.

In Western civilization, at first it was the civil authorities, who had a real interest in preserving order in society and being clear about who owns property and who will inherit that property, but then, as the Roman Empire crumbled, the church began to take control over marriage because Someone (!) needed to oversee the machinations of European royalty and aristocracy and Someone (!) needed to tell all those peasants and commoners how to behave. And so, in 774, the pope presented Charlemagne with a list of rules about legitimate and illegitimate marriage. After all, Someone has to get control over those people out there in the apple orchards!

In subsequent centuries, the church developed marriage liturgies and enlarged the rules governing marriage. One thorny issue that had to be resolved was coming to an agreement on the rules of consanguinity and incest. What if our Joe and our Mary were first cousins? Could their genetic situation overrule their apple orchard vows?

Or what if Joe was already married to someone else in the next village? How about if we start "publishing the Banns" for several weeks before Joe and Mary's public vows so that if someone knows about some extenuating facts about this couple, those facts can be brought to light and the marriage be stopped? (Even today, in many marriage liturgies, a vestige of the ancient Banns appears when the presider says, "If anyone knows any reason why this couple may not be lawfully wedded, speak now or forever hold your peace.")

And since way too many couples are pledging their troth on Saturday evenings on deserted paths, let's start requiring the couple to make their vows in public, before designated witnesses, in front of God and the people, and then—and only then—will they really be married.

And, since we know that young people don't always think clearly and deeply, especially if they are in a hayloft or the backseat of a car, let's require parental consent for marriage at least until the two people are twenty-one years old. Or, maybe twenty-five. Or maybe even thirty.

Finally, at the Fourth Lateran Council in 1215, marriage was declared a sacrament. Interestingly, it was considered to be "the least important sacrament" but marriage was now clearly under the purview of the church. Canon lawyers were unleashed to begin compiling ecclesiastical laws that would enable authorities to settle all disputes. Or at least that was the vision and the hope as the Middle Ages reached its climax and the great cathedrals of Europe stood as a reminder to all about Who Is Really in Charge. But that would all soon change.

With the arrival of the Protestant Reformation, many traditions were challenged, including those undergirding marriage. Not only was the Reformation an earthquake in terms of power and authority in the rising nation states, but Protestant theologians threw a spiritual bomb right at the massive architecture of medieval marriage. Basing their belief and action on the revelation of Scripture (*sola Scriptura*), Martin Luther and the other pioneer Reformers insisted that marriage was not a sacrament. Not only not the least of the sacraments, but no sacrament at all. Sure, Jesus attended a wedding at Cana and helped out with the beverage situation at the reception, but that doesn't make it a sacrament. Then, while the Reformers were at it, they tossed out the sacramental traditions of confession/absolution, ordination, unction, and anything else that couldn't be justified clearly in Scripture.

Down with all of that stuff, said the Reformers. Marriage is good and holy. As a matter of fact, it didn't take Martin Luther very long to enter into marriage after he threw off his monk's garb and freed himself from the rule of the pope and all those ecclesiastical rules. Furthermore, the Protestants taught that sexual intercourse is not the defiling thing that all those prelates had been teaching for so many years. But, no matter how important and good and holy and enjoyable marriage is, it is not a sacrament and it is not something that the church should be controlling.

Waiting in the wings in this historical drama were the new nations that were forming on the crumbling foundation of medieval feudalism. So, when the Reformers in Protestant countries were detaching marriage from church control, the civil authorities in the nation states were there to take over the legal power and authority. The Reformers still wanted to assert moral authority over marriage, but they wanted to get out of the business of actually overseeing the details of marriage.

In this much too cursory overview of the relation of church and state in terms of marriage in the Middle Ages, one thing is particularly noteworthy: most people felt that marriage needed to be controlled but were not clear about who should do the controlling. Back and forth the pendulum swung, from civil oversight to church oversight then back to the civil authorities. In our developing portrait of marriage, we would have to add a civil magistrate to the original scene of Joe and Mary, but then we would have to cover that civil authority with the picture of a priest, only to replace the priest with a justice of the peace or some such functionary of the state.

The fact that a modern clergyperson in the United States is licensed as an officer of the state is a dramatic symbol of this very messy tradition of society trying to decide who will authorize or validate or bless or certify a marriage as being valid and to pronounce, finally, that these two people are in fact, from this time on, married. That this detail in our marriage portrait has been changed so often in the past and continues to be under much discussion in the present is evidence that this particular pendulum has not stopped swinging and this tradition is far from being settled.

Toward the end of the wonderful movie *African Queen*, Mr. Allnut (Humphrey Bogart) and Rosie Sayer (Katharine Hepburn) have finished their dramatic journey down the river, where they battled leeches, mosquitoes, waterfalls, and German gunners. Eventually, they are captured by the Germans and hauled on board a large ship. Just before their scheduled execution, the couple asks the captain of the ship (Theodore Bikel) to marry them. Maybe that would be the best picture to have at this point in this history. Here are two heroic people who have already consented to and consummated their deep and abiding relationship, much to the surprise of both of them, but in the end, they still want some sort of official validation of their marriage, even if it comes from the captain of an enemy ship. They had experienced the joy of companionship and the joy of sex, but now they wanted the joy—even for just a few minutes—of having their marriage officially blessed.

It is not an unusual desire for folks to have, and that is why it is so embedded in our traditions of marriage.

7

MARRIAGE AS A SECULAR CONTRACT

"Marriage is outside the church.... It is a civil matter, and therefore should belong to the government.... We have enough work in our proper office," Martin Luther declared.[17]

As the church lurched its way through the Reformation, huge changes were made regarding marriage, especially concerning who had authority over authorizing and overseeing it. In de-emphasizing the sacramental nature of marriage, the Reformers paved the way for a new emphasis on marriage as a secular reality.

However, this reality was nothing new. It was just a reversion to the pre-Christian tradition adhered to in slightly different forms by Judaism, Greek culture, and Roman law. That tradition held that marriage is not a sacred matter. In fact, the ancient Hebrew prophets were adamant in wanting to distinguish their tradition from the Canaanite fertility cults in which sexual intercourse within marriage was a sacred reenactment of the sexual congress between the father-god and the mother-goddess. The prophets proclaimed that Yahweh needed no female consort and, certainly, unlike the Canannite worship rituals, Yahweh was not to be worshipped with the assistance of temple prostitutes.

One can argue that in their effort to help Yahweh's people resist the allure of the fertility cults, the prophets overreacted and gave us a theological tradition that is needlessly patriarchal in its vision of God. But in terms of marriage, we have inherited the Hebrew notion that it is the couple themselves who make the marriage, unaided by priest or Temple. And the sexual intercourse that binds them together is part of God's good creation, is meant for the couple's delight, and, unlike what those Canaanites down the road believed they were doing, is not a ritualistic link to the fertility of the earth.

As the Protestants reclaimed the tradition of marriage as basically a secular reality, they were able to join hands, figuratively and philosophically, with prominent thinkers of the day, especially John Locke and Jean Jacques Rousseau, who were rebelling against medieval political theory by emphasizing the "social contract" theory of government. And, as Americans know, if the contract is not producing good results, that is, if colonies are stuck with a tyrannical monarch, then it is one's duty to cancel that contract, rebel against the tyrant, and start over with a better contract.

With this point of view becoming preeminent at the time of the Reformation, it doesn't take much imagination to see what some people might call a "slippery slope" in terms of marriage being a contract that can be cancelled. Luther and Calvin and other Protestant leaders did not like divorce, but by shifting the responsibility for marriage to the civil authorities, they did help to pave the road that eventually would take some modern couples to Reno and "quickie divorces."

In France, when they got around to their revolution, this new emphasis on marriage as secular—or this reclaiming of an old emphasis—led to the mandate that couples had to have a civil ceremony because, indeed, it is the state that marries you and it certainly is not God who marries you.

Meanwhile, over in the English colonies, a new form of marriage, called "common law marriage," was being recognized. The thinking was that if two people have lived together and acted as if they were married, the law might as well recognize them as being married. This is the ultimate step in the move toward marriage as a secular contract, because it means that the contract is basically an invisible one (no piece of paper with signatures can be produced, but it is still legally valid in the eyes of the civil authorities and by many people in the community).

This notion of "marriage-as-contract" may be a bit too flexible for some people but this tradition did accomplish some important things. For example, it did enable a married woman to claim a higher degree of justice. In eighteenth-century England, where, by law, the husband and wife were seen as "one person," and the wife's property and legal rights were taken over by the husband ("coverture"), this new idea that the woman had independent legal rights was no small thing.

Furthermore, this concept became the basis for a person to resist the tyranny of an abusive partner. In fact, even before the Reformation, the Roman Catholic Church's insistence on the full consent of both parties to the marriage actually had the revolutionary effect of giving women more rights in the establishment of the marriage bond. Marriage-as-contract may not be very romantic, especially when we envision a portrait of two unhappy people arriving in divorce court, but at least it established a foundation on which a somewhat more just and equitable solution might come out of a tragic situation.

As the pendulum swung toward marriage as a secular reality, there still remained another tradition that paralleled the "contract" tradition. Deeply rooted in Scripture and in the Jewish/Christian experience was the idea of marriage as a covenant.

8

MARRIAGE AS A SACRED COVENANT

Parties to a contract negotiate its terms; each leads from a position of relative strength, even if the qualities of the two strengths be unequal. . . . But in the Yahweh-Israel covenant there was no negotiating, no setting of terms by Israel, no claiming injustice by either. The relationship began with an act of self-giving, rescuing love on the part of Yahweh."[18]

The fundamental experience of the ancient Hebrew people was that they had been liberated from bondage by a unique God who had chosen them and loved them. The relationship between this God and this people was a covenantal relationship in which God took the graceful initiative to bring the people "out of the house of slavery" (Exod. 20:1) and then expected the people to be faithful as a result of this mighty act of deliverance. Unfortunately, the people were less than faithful, a track record dutifully and sorrowfully documented by Moses and the prophets in the collection of books known variously as the Old Testament or the Old

Covenant or the First Covenant or the Hebrew Bible or Tanakh (including Torah, Prophets, Writings).

At the heart of Hebrew Scripture—and later Christian Scripture—is the concept of "covenant." The word occurs more than three hundred times in the Bible, but there is never a precise definition given for it. Instead, we come to understand it through the stories that are told about it. One of the most dramatic stories is the story of Hosea and Gomer.

Today, using our modern categories of psychology, we might say that Hosea was "obsessed" by Gomer, who was a "loose woman," a harlot who became Hosea's unfaithful spouse. In describing his heart-breaking and poignant relationship with Gomer, Hosea is also describing Yahweh's relationship to Yahweh's "spouse" (that is, the Hebrew people) who had been every bit as unfaithful to their covenant with God as Gomer was unfaithful to her covenant with Hosea. Yet, the good news proclaimed by the prophet Hosea is that God would not give up on the people. Because Yahweh is motivated by *hesed* (steadfast love), God would not let them go unloved. They might decide to break the covenant again and again and again, but it would be broken from the human side, not the divine side.

In the New Testament, we read the story of how the same loving God who created the world and humankind and who liberated the Hebrew people acted in a new way. The Word of Creation and Liberation became incarnate in Jesus of Nazareth. The Gospels tell the story of *Hesed*-Becoming-Human and how this Word-Become-Flesh was "heard, . . . seen . . . looked at and touched with our hands" (1 John 1:1). The story of Jesus' blood becoming the sign of a new covenant is retold and reenacted on Sundays and other days when Christians gather to celebrate what the Creator/Liberator God has done and continues to do in the world. The steadfastness and lovingkindness of God's commitment to humankind is at the heart of this notion of covenant. God's love for the people is undying:

- "I have loved you with an everlasting love; therefore I have continued my faithfulness to you" (Jer. 31:3).

- "I will remember my covenant with you in the days of your youth, and I will establish with you an everlasting covenant" (Ezek. 16:60).
- "For a brief moment I abandoned you, but with great compassion I will gather you. In overflowing wrath for a moment I hid my face from you, but with everlasting love I will have compassion on you, says the Lord, your Redeemer" (Isa. 54:7–8).

A very impressive display of where this God is coming from! Inevitably, as the prophets searched for metaphors to describe this divine *hesed*, they turned to marriage scenes.

- "For as a young man marries a young woman, so shall your builder marry you, and as the bridegroom rejoices over the bride, so shall your God rejoice over you" (Isa. 62:5).
- "Come, my beloved, let us go forth into the fields, and lodge in the villages; let us go out early to the vineyards, and see whether the vines have budded, whether the grape blossoms have opened and the pomegranates are in bloom. There I will give you my love" (Song of Songs 7:11–12).

When the early Christians were forming their communities and trying to articulate their experience of God's *hesed*, it is again not surprising that it is to the vocabulary of marriage that the writers turned. For example, in the letter to the Ephesians, there is the (in)famous passage (Eph. 5:21–6:8) that makes many moderns cringe because of its alleged partriarchalism ("Wives, be subject to your husbands . . ."). However, it is very important to read this passage carefully and completely to see that it is all about the mutual subordination of husband and wife, parents and children, and masters and slaves. The model for Christian behavior, especially in marriage, is the life of Jesus, who incarnated true servanthood and nondomination. Or, to put it in other words, marriage is founded on the "great mystery" of God's loving relationship with God's people and the loving relationship between Christ and the church.

At the very end of the Bible, in the strange book entitled "The Revelation to John," the enraptured author has a vision of the end time, when God consummates the relationship that began in creation and liberation and continued through incarnation. What language does this inspired writer use to try to describe the climax of all history and experience? "Then I saw a new heaven and a new earth; for the first heaven and the first earth had passed away, and the sea was no more. And I saw the holy city, the new Jerusalem, coming down out of heaven from God, prepared as a bride adorned for her husband" (Rev. 21:1–2). There may be some objection to this still patriarchal image of God-as-husband, but one could certainly do worse in terms of metaphors than this description of a divine wedding as the beginning of a whole new way of living

If *hesed* is at the heart of divine reality and relationship, then it also becomes the heart of human reality and relationship, especially that sacred human relationship called marriage. "Contract" is never enough when it comes to marriage. "Covenant" takes us to our biblical roots and begins to describe the deepest experience that any human can have—the experience of being loved steadfastly and unconditionally and then trying to reciprocate that love. We humans never quite get this kind of relationship right, but God does. And that gives us tremendous cause for hope and can keep us on the road to fidelity and mutuality and steadfast commitment in times that are sometimes better and sometimes worse and at times when we are sick or well or rich or poor.

For those who experience themselves as called by God to a marriage relationship, their reality is much more than a contract. It is a sacred covenant, which means that a portrait of this tradition of marriage requires that some symbol of sacredness be incorporated into the picture. The symbols available are manifold and do not necessarily involve the presence of a clergyperson—just something to represent the presence of God in this union.

9

BETROTHAL

Troth n. 1. faith; fidelity; pledged faith, as in plighted troth 2. truth or verity 3. *Archaic* Betrothal[19]

It is a natural step to go from meditating on God's promise of faithfulness to considering human attempts to be faithful in a marriage relationship. For many people, this attempt begins with betrothal, when two people indeed pledge to be loyal or faithful one to another.

In some marriage liturgies, such as the 1928 Book of Common Prayer, this pledge occurs early in the service. In spite of the countless Hollywood movie wedding scenes in which a bride and groom say, "I do," the fact is that in many church liturgies, the key phrase is "I will." Significantly, this is a pledge about the future, not a statement about the present (notwithstanding that a couple will often spend a huge amount of cash in order to have a very dramatic experience in that wedding moment!).

In the past, this promise about the future was often made at the time of what we might call "engagement," but as we have already seen, the traditional institution of betrothal was actually closer to being married than not being married. The use of the word "espoused" in some translations of Matthew 1:18 catches our attention because it calls to mind our word "spouse," which is clearly a term describing marriage. In point of fact, if we revisit the customs that existed at the time of Joseph and Mary in first-century Galilee, we can fairly say that they were "legally married."

As we read Matthew's description of the decision Joseph had to make when he found out that Mary was pregnant, we realize Joseph would have to take legal action, that is, divorce, if he decided to "dismiss her" (Matt. 1:19). The fact that Joseph "stood by his woman" and did not pursue divorce was a dramatic instance of someone repudiating his patriarchal entitlements in favor of a greater good. Had Joseph chosen otherwise, he would have been required to break the betrothal through divorce—which indicates how substantial a commitment had been made.

The plot thickens a bit as we ask the obvious question: Did the betrothal of two first-century Jews confer on them the right of sexual intercourse? If they were indeed as good as married, wouldn't they be permitted to have all the rights and pleasures of marriage? Ah, good questions. But let's not hold our breath waiting for an answer from scholars. The best answer seems to be, "Maybe so, maybe not." As one modern scholar says, "We can be confident that the assumption that betrothal periods at the time of Mary and Joseph did not include sexual intimacy owes more to an idealization of the facts than to the facts themselves."[20]

Taking a quick detour around the issue of first-century Jewish betrothal/sexual customs, let's catch our breath and set out on the road that is marked the "Nuptial Process." Our Jewish ancestors had great insight into the human condition. They realized that marriage is not a one-magic-moment event. Instead, marriage was seen as a process, sometimes begun by an arrangement between two families, which is what happened with Isaac and Rebekah and Jacob and Leah/Rachel, but at other times begun by mutual consent of the two people themselves. A similar process existed in the imperial Roman culture in which the early church was established and grew. Because they inherited Jewish and Roman models of betrothal, it is not surprising that the early

Christians adopted the practice and formulated liturgies for this important time in the long process of becoming married.

Surrounded and supported by their family, friends, and community, couples who embarked on the nuptial process moved gradually into a deeper and deeper relationship with each other as they went through three major stages called betrothal, consummation, and benediction (which, for religious people, was the final sealing of the marriage bond). Like the stages of grief, these stages of the ancient nuptial process were not neat and tidy. Depending on the era and the culture, each couple negotiated the stages of becoming married in their own particular and idiosyncratic way.

However, in spite of the manifold differences, the tradition of betrothal reminds us that marriage is a process, not an accomplishment, a journey, not a destination. Like all human endeavors, the nuptial process was—and still is—a fairly messy process. In our contemporary culture, as the average age of puberty falls, as the average age of marriage rises, and as the divorce rate continues at a high rate, we could say that couples who live together or cohabit before a wedding ceremony are basically reclaiming the ancient tradition of betrothal.

Unlike our Christian forebears, we have not developed public acknowledgments for this important time in the life of a couple. The observation "Oh, did you hear that Joe and Mary are living together?" doesn't quite have the same weight as our ancestors' formal betrothal events.

Not surprisingly, many church leaders, ethicists, marriage counselors, and Christian writers are currently recommending that Christians retrieve the ancient tradition of betrothal as a way to help couples steer their way through the nuptial process without depending solely on the advice of modern bridal magazines and the services of high-priced wedding planners. Reclaiming the tradition of betrothal is one way to invite couples to embark on a long process of continuous pledging of fidelity and a steadfast commitment to a process of mutual growth and forbearance.

The marriage portrait in front of us at this point shows a couple looking out at a long and winding road. It's a simple painting, with muted colors. The road disappears into the distance and the lines are a bit blurry where the land meets the sky. All we see are the couple's backs. The central feature of the portrait is their hands tightly clasped together. Next to the road is a small, neatly lettered sign that says, "Betrothal."

Next to this portrait are some glossy photographs, a display of brochures, and a lot of advertisements from the modern wedding industry. The photos show various "beautiful settings" with flower-strewn aisles waiting for the arrival of a resplendent bride, who will soon meet her groom and experience their "magic wedding moment." In one large photograph, off to the side but still plainly visible, is a string quartet. Off to the other side is a view of a large hall, full of tables set for a fine dinner. Attached to the corner of this huge display is a price tag on which are written the words: "Estimated price: $25,000." That price tag reminds us that we are in a new and quite expensive world in terms of what is important in marriage.

10

MODERN MARRIAGE

For several millennia, marriage was essentially about property and procreation. Put another way, marriage was about making money and making babies. Only in the modern era, in industrialized Western countries, has marriage made a fundamental departure from the tradition of "getting hitched" for economic and kinship purposes.

UNHITCHING MARRIAGE FROM PROPERTY AND PROCREATION

People often got married in order to form an economic partnership, either through inheriting family wealth or through joining forces to earn a living. In nonaristocratic families, the husband (original term: "house-bound") needed a wife, who could add to the economic well-being of the family by becoming an "ale wife" or a "fish wife" or a "mid-wife" in order to make the couple more economically self-sufficient. The wife, of course, was also expected to keep house, mend the clothing, and fix the food.

The other thing that women did, of course, was have babies. Child-bearing was of the essence of marriage. It insured the continuation of the family and clan, and it also provided more workers for all the chores on the farm and in the house. In addition, children gave their parents some social security, because they guaranteed that there would be someone to care for the old folks who could no longer "tow the barge and lift the bale."

But all of that changed when industrialization undercut the essentially rural culture and economy of the West. Jobs were no longer primarily on farms, but were in factories, mines, mills, and shops. In this brave new world, husbands had to leave home to go to work, while wives became the ones who were "house-bound." They had to rear the children, but didn't get much help from their husbands, who were working far away from home. Gradually, children became more of a burden than an asset. Instead of being contributors to the family "industry," they became mouths to feed.

These historical currents swept away some key underpinnings of the ancient traditions of marriage. Property and procreation were no longer at the center of marital arrangements. Two other modern developments further undercut the institution of marriage as it had existed for hundreds and hundreds of years: birth control and women's education.

In the nineteenth century, some fairly primitive methods of birth control, including "herbal contraceptives," Vaseline, and Lysol, enabled women and men to have much more choice about conception and procreation. Not too far in the future was the Pill, which would assure many women that they would have a high degree of control over conception. A song by Loretta Lynn illustrates the dramatic change this caused in the twentieth century: "All these years I've stayed at home/while you had all your fun./ And every year that's gone by/another baby's come./There's gonna be some changes made/right here on Nursery Hill./You've set your chickens your last time,/'cause now I've got the Pill."[21]

This new reality of birth control, of course, set off a firestorm of moralistic campaigns, beginning in the late nineteenth century with the effort of Anthony Comstock to criminalize distribution of articles for the prevention of conception. Many states passed "Defense of Decency" and "Defense of

Marriage" legislation. Having babies by choice and not by obligation? Horrors! What is the world coming to? What is happening to "traditional marriage?"

But as soon as procreation became a choice and not a requirement within marriage, especially in America, the new pioneers were not the folks in covered wagons heading west, but people like Margaret Sanger, who were giving women new power to control their own bodies and their own lives in a way that would have been unimaginable to their parents, grandparents, and other ancestors. In the process, marriage was unhitched from procreation forever.

At the same time that women were given the chance to live their lives unbound from the unrelenting demands of pregnancy, childbirth, and child-rearing, they also took their places in classrooms where they had not been welcome previously. For example, from 1890 until 1910 in the United States, female college enrollment tripled. There was huge resistance to this development. One influential physician conveniently linked these two "revolutions"—birth control and women's education—in an amazing piece of writing. Try to keep a straight face as you read the following:

"Serious education for women will . . . derange the tides of her organization . . . divert blood from the reproductive apparatus to the head . . . and bring on dysmennorrhea, chronic and acute ovaritis, prolapsed uteri, hysteria, neuralgia, and the like."[22]

Who is the really hysterical one in this scene? But, of course, hysteria is always the reaction when "traditional marriage" (or at least some people's notion of "traditional marriage") is threatened. Out come the Bibles. Up on the soapboxes and into the pulpits go the righteous defenders of marriage. These things must be stopped! Man the barricades (and "man" is often the appropriate verb in these situations)! The ferocity of those late-nineteenth- and early-twentieth-century campaigns to oppose birth control and resist women's emancipation (including women's right to vote) serves as evidence to show that once again in human history a new tradition of marriage was evolving.

The choices for a portrait for this era of marriage are almost too numerous to consider. Should we show a picture of Margaret

Sanger's first birth control clinic in Brooklyn's Brownsville district in 1916? Should we show a photo of eager women college students at Wellesley or Smith or Bryn Mawr? Or, just to really dramatize how things were changing, how about a portrait of a single woman with lipstick and bobbed hair, doing the Charleston with a cigarette in her mouth? As the famous modern advertisement trumpeted, "You've come a long way, baby!"

And the fact that in none of these pictures is a man present shows us what a huge leap forward was taken, with major ramifications for the traditions of marriage.

WOMEN'S EQUALITY

In a book devoted to exploring the traditions of Western marriage, it may seem strange to begin this section with the story of a twelve-year-old Maori girl, but by recalling the marvelous film entitled *Whale Rider*, we may be able to put the tradition of women's equality within marriage in a larger context. That context, of course, is patriarchy, a reality that has been deeply embedded in many cultures and institutions, including our own, for many millennia.

In *Whale Rider*, we are treated to the wonderful and poignant story of Pai, the female twin of a brother who died, along with their mother, during childbirth. Her brother was going to be heir to the leadership of the Ngati Konohi people. Grief-stricken and heart-broken, Pai's father flees from his home and family and leaves Pai to be raised by her grandfather, who becomes the symbol of unrelenting, unbending patriarchy. The grandfather's refusal to allow Pai to become a leader—and Pai's own insistence on claiming her own identity and vocation—is the focus for this compelling drama.

In the climactic scene of the film, when Pai mounts a huge beached whale and rides it back out to sea, can we see the whale as a symbol of a patriarchal tradition that had become exhausted and was depleting the tribe of life? In order for new life to be infused into the tribe, the patriarch had to repent. Like the huge whale, the grandfather had to turn around and go in a different direction, with Pai as the leader and life-bringer.

Taking a huge leap in culture, geography, and time, we can go directly from Pai's struggle to claim her rights within her Maori tribe to nineteenth-century America and four women who also confronted patriarchy, including its manifestation within the institution of marriage. The four women are Elizabeth Cady Stanton, Amelia Jenks Bloomer, Sojourner Truth, and Harriet Tubman.

In the Episcopal Church's book *Lesser Feasts and Fasts*, we find thumbnail sketches of these four remarkable women. They were all prophets in the best sense of that word. They spoke truth to power, especially male power. It is sad that the Episcopal Church has chosen to lump these four women together on one "feast day" (July 20), for like Pai, each of them has a unique story, and each of them could be the basis of a fine film and a feast day of her own. For the purposes of this book, let's focus on portraits of just the first two.

Elizabeth Cady Stanton "dedicated her life to righting the wrongs perpetrated upon women by the church and society."[23] She and four other women organized the first Women's Rights Convention in Seneca Falls, New York, on July 19–20, 1848. That conference marked the beginning of Stanton's fifty-year effort to hold the church accountable for "oppressing women by using Scripture to enforce subordination of women in marriage and to prohibit them from ordained ministry."[24]

The resistance Stanton and her colleagues experienced was similar to what little Pai experienced in her grandfather's obstinacy. Yet Stanton would not get off this whale. She persevered. She insisted on fighting discrimination against women, including the male bias and misogyny that had infiltrated the work of Bible translation. She and some colleagues produced *The Woman's Bible* in the 1890s as one specific way to counteract patriarchy and begin the effort to read Scripture from a feminist perspective.

Joining Stanton in critiquing the church and its Scriptures for the way that women were treated, Amelia Jenks Bloomer is remembered best for the way that she influenced a change in women's clothing customs. "Faith and fashion collided explosively when she published in her newspaper, *The Lily*, a picture of herself in loose-fitting Turkish trousers, and began wearing them publicly."[25] In her rebellion against the constricting corsets of her time, Bloomer was also rebelling against the patriarchal control of women in the church, in society, and also in marriage

And we certainly have not heard the last explosion in this ongoing struggle by women to claim equality in all aspects of life. As I began writing this particular section of the book, the newspapers and magazines were full of stories about a speech given by Lawrence H. Summers, then the president of Harvard University. Addressing the National Board of Economic Research, Mr. Summers contended that women might be less inclined to advance to top levels in science and mathematics because they are not as committed as men to the hard work necessary to succeed and because they seem to have some "innate differences" that might account for the relative paucity of women in top academic jobs in these fields.

Can we see a link between Summers' speech, the fiery denunciations that Stanton and Bloomer had to endure, the hysterical rant against education for women referred to in the previous section, and the terse comments from Pai's grandfather in *Whale Rider* about how girls just aren't as good as boys? Each example has its own particular context, but isn't the larger context still the same—the effort to diminish women? This book, as it paints with very broad brush strokes, cannot do justice to this complex topic, but we can at least imagine a portrait of Elizabeth Cady Stanton, a copy of *The Woman's Bible* under one arm while the other arm is linked with the arm of Amelia Jenks Bloomer, who is standing comfortably and proudly in her loose-fitting Turkish trousers.

Looking at this portrait, can anyone deny that these two women symbolize how marriage in the United States was going to take a major turn and head out into some very deep and uncharted waters? And we are a long way from coming to any ending to this particular story.

MARRYING FOR LOVE

Love and marriage, love and marriage,
go together like a horse and carriage,

this I tell ya, brother,
ya can't have one without the other.[26]

In *Fiddler on the Roof*, we have an excellent example of a very "traditional" marriage from the past—a marriage arranged for the couple by their families, a marriage based on a partnership for economic survival, and a marriage centered on the procreation and rearing of children. But toward the end of the play, Tevye sits next to Golde and sings, "Do you love me?" She replies, "Do I *WHAT?*"

The song goes on to explore the possibility that, after being married for twenty-five years, their marriage has become bound together by more than practical economics and producing children. Wistfully, and somewhat impatiently, Golde sings, "Yes, I suppose I do."

Then Tevye and Golde end the song together, singing the words, "After twenty-five years . . . it's nice to know."

In chapter 2 of this book, we noted that the first biblical description of marriage was the one between Isaac and Rebekah. It was an arranged marriage, similar to that of Tevye and Golde, and its purposes were the classic ones, including the need to perpetuate the tribe. However, in the text of the story, we can be gladdened to find that Isaac "took Rebekah and she became his wife; and he loved her" (Gen. 24:67). But, like Tevye and Golde's experience, this love seems to be more serendipitous than necessary. In each case, the marriage would have taken place, regardless of the feelings the two people had for each other.

For most of the history of marriage, love was not at the center. It might happen. It might not. But it was not essential, especially at the beginning of the relationship. As one scholar noted in his analysis of ancient Rome, "Love in marriage was a stroke of good fortune; it was not the basis of the institution."[27]

In our modern experience, we seem to have taken a 180-degree turn. With economic and procreative purposes being less important, especially for relatively affluent or middle-class, well-educated couples, love has moved to the center of the marriage portrait. Modern couples, inspired by popular songs and movies and literature, expect to "fall in love" and then get married. If marriage has become unhitched from property and procreation, it has dramatically become hitched to love. Love and marriage, as the song says, go together like a horse and carriage.

But this is a very new tradition. It is difficult to know exactly what Isaac and Rebekah experienced in what the text of Genesis calls "love." They left us no diaries or letters or transcripts of their most intimate conversations, so we do not know the texture of their experience of love. Today, the word "love" in its popular usage usually connotes a complex mixture of infatuation, sexual passion, psychological obsession, emotional attachment, and sentimental commitment. This is what sells, whether it be via CDs or cinema or novels or Valentine's Day cards. This love is very sweet, highly sentimental, and often sexual. As one commentator suggests, maybe it would be better to term this experience and reality, especially in its commercialized form, "luv."

> To turn love into "luv," you eliminate from love everything that seems ambiguous or dark or negative. You omit to mention that love profoundly challenges our self-centeredness: you don't remind people that the commitment that goes with real love is real commitment. You certainly don't hint that genuine relationships of love contain a high degree of honesty and the readiness to confront differences. And above all, you never suggest that (to quote a phrase!) "the line between love and hate is as thin as a razor's edge." Never will you find that sentiment or anything remotely resembling it on a (drugstore) greeting card.[28]

Did Isaac and Rebekah, or Golde and Tevye, experience "luv"? Maybe. Maybe not. What seems more accurate to say is that these couples experienced "love" as defined by James Thurber: "Love is what you've been through with somebody." Whether it be in the ancient hills of Canaan or the village of Anatevka or on the Congo River where Mr. Alnutt and Rosie went through so much together, the kind of "love" we see portrayed in those stories is quite different from the pictures of "luv" that are hawked these days in America.

In the Judeo-Christian experience, our understanding of love is founded on the experience of God, the Divine Lover, whose relationship with us is dramatically different from the erotic and sentimental love that sells cars and movies and fuels Valentines' Day celebrations. It is the steadfast love of God, which the Hebrew word *hesed* and the Greek word *agape* try to describe, that is our ultimate model of love. It is that divine love, bound up as it is with indomitable commitment to and willingness to suffer for the Beloved, that helps us begin to understand what our overused English word "love" means.

Whether it be "luv" or "love," though, modern couples usually don't have much choice in terms of their expectations for marriage. Love and marriage, indeed, are now inextricably mixed. In former times, two people would pledge to be faithful to their marriage vows "so long as we both shall live." In our modern marrying, do we find the implicit (or explicit?) assumption underlying the vows to be "so long as we both shall *love*"?

Those words might be on a banner stretched overhead in the portrait of a happy couple looking at each other as they make their vows. That banner would be a good reminder of a major change in focus for modern marriages. Marriages today are being built on a very different foundation, especially if the couple expects to leave their wedding and "live happily ever after." That fairy tale ending is very attractive and highly motivating in the run-up to nuptial ceremonies. But what happens when the couple wakes up one morning and one or both of them feel that they aren't "happy?"

MARRYING FOR HAPPINESS

"There is no happiness; there are only moments of happiness" (Spanish proverb).

In 2002, a young woman named Pamela Paul published a book entitled *The Starter Marriage and the Future of Matrimony*. The author had dated a man for eighteen months and then spent a year planning their 1998 wedding. Their marriage broke up three weeks before their first anniversary. The divorce inspired Paul to examine why as many as 25 percent of first marriages in America fail within two years. She interviewed sixty Gen-Xers (people born between 1965 and 1978), couples whose marriages had lasted five years or fewer and had ended without children.

Pamela Paul makes no claims to having done exhaustive research on this demographic phenomenon that she calls "starter marriages," but she does raise some fascinating questions and makes some intriguing observations about marriages in which the participants spent more time—and money—planning the wedding than they did in the marriage itself.

One conclusion she draws from her interviews and that led to the title of her book is that these couples may be better prepared for a second marriage. As she said in an interview after the book was published, "About a third of my subjects have remarried, and they say they felt much better prepared. A starter marriage is like a starter home: When you leave it, you're going to make sure with the next one that the basement is finished and the insulation is in place."[29]

Comparing one's second husband to a house with a finished basement and good insulation may not be the most romantic idea or exciting metaphor, but Ms. Paul at least cuts through a lot of the "matrimania" hype that leads too many young couples into marriage, only to find themselves waking up on the day after the wedding without many clues as to what they will do next.

Pamela Paul zeros in on the couples' lack of preparedness by noting that many of the parents of these young people often made no judgment about their children's marriages (possibly because many of the parents are divorced themselves) and apparently gave little or no advice about marriage beyond telling their children at the time of engagement that the parents just wanted the couple to "be happy."

If that is the premarital advice that a bride and groom receive, no wonder they wake up to an empty feeling after the wedding is over. Of course, parents want their children to be happy. Similarly, parents want their children to be well fed, but if the children are only given cotton candy to eat, they will have very little nutrition and nothing to stick to their ribs. Or, to use Pamela Paul's metaphor, if the basement is not ready for occupancy and there is no insulation in the walls, there is unhappiness and discomfort on the horizon.

As much as moralists like to point the finger at the laxity and self-indulgence of the baby boomer generation from which these couples' parents came or at the shallowness of the couples themselves, the real culprit here is the assumption that marriage will make a couple "happy." That assumption is deeply imbedded in our culture's traditions of marriage, and the portrait that probably captures that tradition best is any photo of the smiling bride and groom sailing down the steps of a church with bridal veil fluttering, tuxedo jacket flapping, and hands held up half-heartedly to ward off the rice or bubbles in the air. The caption for this photo could be "Happily Ever After," which would alert us to the fact that it is more of a fairy tale than a picture of reality. Just ask some of Ms. Paul's interviewees—-and their parents—about the "ever after" part.

The Spanish proverb opening this chapter is certainly not fairy tale language. It alerts prospective husbands and wives to the fact that their wedding will not guarantee much of anything—certainly not happiness. When Thomas Jefferson penned the Declaration of Independence, he included in the preamble the notion that life in the United States would be based on life, liberty, and the pursuit of happiness. Mr. Jefferson, whose own marital history we briefly examined in an earlier chapter, wisely did not say that happiness would be secured by a new political arrangement. He simply said that the new country would be set up in such a way that more people could "pursue" happiness (which in Jefferson's mind probably meant the accumulation of property, including slaves).

In a similar way, in modern Western affluent cultures (it is worth noting that most of the couples in Ms. Paul's survey were white, college-educated, and fairly well off), marriage is often seen as the way to pursue happiness. Unhitched from procreation and economic necessity, modern marriage has often drifted into the ethereal, cotton-candy realm of "luv" and "Happily Ever After." My brief description of this modern tradition of marriage-for-the-purpose-of-happiness is not meant to deride either marriage or happiness. It is merely documenting the fact that this is quite a new tradition. In ages past, people did not primarily marry for the sake of happiness. They rejoiced, of course, in the moments of happiness that occurred, but they generally did not base their marriage on the assumption that they would achieve a permanent state that could be termed "happiness."

In my own meditation on this fragile reality called "happiness," I am drawn to a story I heard years ago. It is about a young kitten that was always chasing its own tail. 'Round and 'round it would go, never quite latching on to that elusive object that seemed so close yet was so far away. One day, an older cat walked past the frantically circling kitten and asked, "What are you doing?"

The kitten replied, "I'm trying to catch my tail. If I can catch it, I will be very happy."

The old cat looked with compassion on the kitten and said, "I did the same thing when I was younger, but then I found that if I just went about my business, my tail would follow right along behind me."

This story is more of a homiletical illustration than a piece of historical evidence, but it does dovetail with the experience of couples who are not counseled about how to deal with the conflicts and disappointments and inevitable ups and downs of marriage. If couples follow the modern tradition of marriage, they may be more like the young kitten, frantically pursuing something that can't be caught. The old cat seems to know a deeper tradition that has to do more with vocation ("going about one's business") and savoring the moments of happiness that will inevitably follow.

But the language of vocation, accompanied as it is by notions of self-sacrifice, suffering, and deep commitment, is not the language that underpins the modern wedding industry. That very profitable industry is selling happiness. Lots and lots of happiness.

The sad reality that we are facing, especially as people live longer, is that a marriage that is not well insulated or built on a solid foundation will be like the house in Matthew 7:27—built on sand. The rain falls and the floods come and the winds blow and beat against that house, and it falls—and great is its fall. Which means we need to spend a bit of time on the modern tradition of divorce.

ENDING MARRIAGE THROUGH DIVORCE

> Suppose a man enters into a marriage with a woman, but she does not please him because he finds something objectionable about her, and so he writes her a certificate of divorce, puts it in her hand, and sends her out of his house . . ." (Deut. 24:1)

According to three of the Gospel writers, not too long before Jesus was arrested, he was approached by some legal scholars who wanted to put him on the spot. (Failing to do so, some of them apparently helped in the conspiracy to put him on the cross.) These legalists wanted to make Jesus take a position on the legal grounds for divorce, thereby forcing him to ally himself with one specific tradition of interpretation—rather like modern interrogators who try to get a political candidate to be clear about his or her position on an important topic like abortion or same-sex marriage, which then has the effect of alienating the candidate from people who don't hold that particular position.

"Is it lawful for a man to divorce his wife?," asked the legal beagles.

Jesus, as was his wont, then did a neat little tap dance and refused to be boxed in by their question. First, he referred to the Mosaic law (quoted above) that gave men a lot of leeway in the grounds for divorcing their wives. "Something objectionable." It doesn't take a Harvard law degree to back that claim up. Burning the toast for breakfast? Not cleaning the house well enough? Not a virgin at the time of marriage? Not producing the right kind of children? Away with you! Here's your certificate of divorce. So long.

After Jesus directed the legalists' attention to that tradition, he then stood up for women who were treated so very unjustly by this kind of situation, and basically Jesus said, "No divorce is allowed." ("What God has joined together, let no one separate"— Mark 10:9). In making this pronouncement, Jesus not only takes the wind out of the legalists' sails, but he also takes his listeners on a quick little trip through both creation stories in Hebrew Scripture. He references Genesis 1 ("God made them male and female") and then immediately tacks on a few verses from Genesis 2 to celebrate the fact that the first man and the first woman were made one flesh by God.

So much for your divorce customs, fellas, says Jesus. You've got to rethink this whole thing. You've got to look at the Big Picture of what God intends, especially for husbands and wives. But it was hard for the legal scholars of his day to do that. And it was hard for Jesus' own followers to do that. By the time Matthew wrote his Gospel, maybe twenty years after Mark, the church was already struggling with this "hard saying" of Jesus and Matthew included the famous "Matthean exception" in his version of Jesus' teaching. Instead of a flat "No divorce is allowed," Matthew's Jesus says, "Whoever divorces his wife, except for unchastity, and marries another commits adultery" (Matt. 19:9).

By 1849, the state of Connecticut passed a law allowing divorce for "any such misconduct as permanently destroys the happiness of the petitioner and defeats the purposes of the marriage relation."[30] It is a huge leap from the single exception of "unchastity" to the huge exception of "unhappiness," but as society made that leap during the almost two millennia between Matthew's Gospel and Connecticut's court ruling, the church had to grapple with how to resolve the tension between Jesus' vision of the indissolubility of marriage and the reality of humankind's "hardness of heart" (Mark 10:5). That tension is difficult to experience day in and day out when two people try to live with each other for a long time of ups and downs, sickness and health, and richness and poverty, let alone in the course of the many "objectionable things" that each partner discovers about the other in the dailiness of their lives together.

Even the Roman Catholic Church, which for centuries sought to uphold the no-divorce tradition, had to evolve a new tradition of "annulment" in order to provide a way out of marriage for people who clearly were not able to live as "one flesh." By the twentieth century, when the scholars and theologians and canon lawyers of Vatican II opened the windows on marriage and let some fresh air blow in, the reasons for annulment had been expanded to include the following: "lack of discretion (the parties did not really understand what they were committing themselves to), lack of partnership in conjugal life, lack of conjugal love, psychopathic personality, schizophrenia, affective immaturity, psychic incompetence, sociopathic personality, 'moral incompetence,' and lack of interpersonal communication."[31]

Some people may say that the long list of reasons for annulment opens way too many loopholes and goes too far down the road toward the realm of "I'm not happy, so good-bye." But a compassionate look at the tradition of annulment can lead us to at least see it as an effort to deal with the enormous tension between the vision of what marriage ought to be and the reality of being married.

One can see how hard it is to deal with the tension between vision and reality by looking at statistics and graphs that document the divorce rate in the twentieth century in Europe and North America. The chart on the following page are evidence of the bumpy road traveled by married couples in the United States.

Fueled by many factors, including the narrowing down of the purposes for marrying to the indefinable and fragile foundations of "love" and "happiness," modern couples have inherited a relatively new tradition in which divorce, for whatever reason is allowed by civil or religious authorities, is easier to achieve. This modern tradition, graphically portrayed in the table on page 92, shows that in the recent past and in the foreseeable future a large percentage of couples will be parted not by death but by divorce. As Richard Pryor, the late comedian, once said, "Marriage is really tough because you have to deal with feelings and lawyers."[32]

This development in the history of marriage is yet another reminder of how daunting a challenge it is for modern couples to make their marriages thrive and endure. Consideration of this reality can make people very depressed or very angry. It makes some people unrealistically nostalgic for the allegedly "good old days" or self-righteously passionate about "doing something to

Percent of Marriages Ending in Divorce or Separation after 15 Years
(Women, 1995)

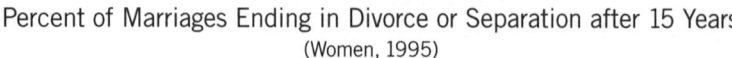

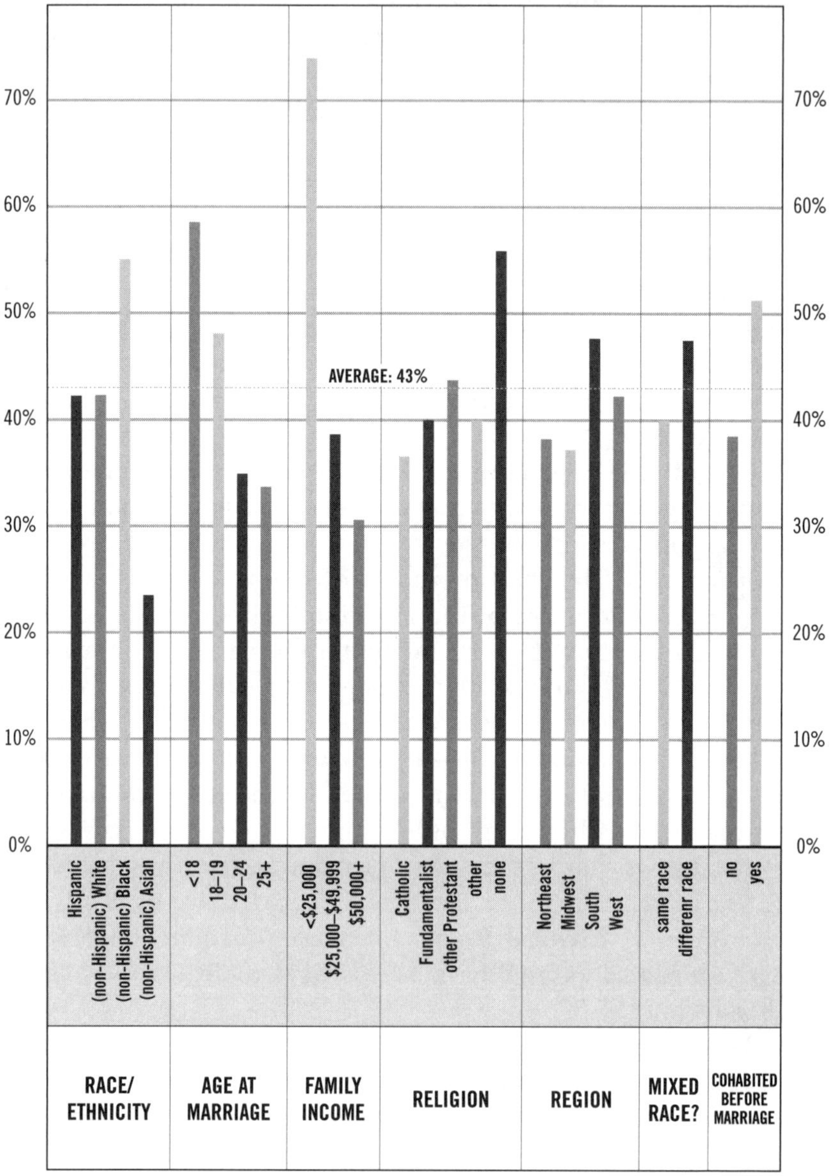

Source: National Center for Health Statistics and U.S. Census Bureau, found in "State of the Union: the Marriage Issue," *The Nation*, 279/1 (July 5, 2004), 27.

reverse this trend." Each of those latter options merits at least a long chapter or referral to some good resources in order to help people understand that for many people the "old days" were not so good and the present days are not so bad. Suffice it to say here that cool heads are needed before ideologues go charging off on their steeds to rescue the fair damsel called "Marriage."

 I certainly would not want to end a brief review of the history of marriage on this somewhat discouraging discussion of divorce. Instead, I think it is important to bring to the surface one final tradition that can be celebrated and might help us take a few steps out of despair and toward cool-headedness. Having done that, we will then be ready to revisit Eden before taking a look at some sketches for a possible new portrait of marriage.

※ II ※

MARRIAGE FOR COMPANIONSHIP

John and Abigail Adams were separated many times during their marriage. At first, John was away from home as he rode the court circuit as a young lawyer; then he was at the Continental Congress in Philadelphia, and, later, in Europe as a representative of the fledgling nation. During this time, Abigail and John exchanged more than a thousand letters, which give us a glimpse into a unique and intimate relationship.

Unlike many marriages of their time, especially those of other "founding fathers," the Adamses established a relationship that was free of much of the prevalent patriarchalism. The fact that they addressed each other as "Dear Partner" and "Dearest Friend" indicates that they had moved beyond the customs of their day in which a husband would commonly refer to his wife as "Dear Child" and she would address him as "Mister." It is not surprising to see this evidence of formality and hierarchy in marital relationships, since this was a time when public records show that women had no real independent legal existence. The laws of "coverture" made women into "the wife of" or "the daughter of" or "the sister of."

In that culture, the relationship of John and Abigail Adams was remarkable. While George Washington and Alexander Hamilton and Thomas Jefferson were using marriage as a way to acquire property and advance socially, the Adamses came to their marriage with an emotional and intellectual compatibility that was discovered during their courtship and continued to bind them together all their lives. Their letters are testimony to the quality of their relationship. Who cannot be moved when they read the following excerpt from Abigail's letter to John while he is at the Continental Congress? She wrote, "I never close my eyes at night till I have been to Philadelphia, and my first visit in the morning is there."[33]

Besides being spouses and lovers, John and Abigail were each other's best friend and intellectual partner. Those who read David McCullough's prize-winning biography of John Adams get a glimpse into this wonderful marriage. Some historians refer to theirs as a "companionate marriage," a term used to describe a marriage in which there is equality and common purpose. It is interesting to note that the term "companionate marriage" has also been used by authors to describe the marriages of Pontius Pilate and his wife, Cole and Linda Lee Porter, and Bill and Hillary Clinton. The diversity of these couples' relationships suggests that the term "companionate marriage" is a fairly broad term!

In recent years, Abigail Adams has become a feminist icon. Her entreaty to John and the other men in Philadelphia to "remember the ladies" was seen as establishing her as a proto-feminist. She certainly deserves credit for speaking out boldly on behalf of women's educational and legal rights, and her ability to manage the family farm and be head of the household in John's absence was remarkable. But it would be unfair to her to suggest that these were the most important accomplishments in her life. She wanted John to return so that they would be together as husband and wife and father and mother to their children. It is that desire that seems to set them apart from some of the other celebrities whose marriages are called "companionate."

This tradition of marriage as a union of two people who are spouses, lovers, friends, and partners is founded on an ideal relationship in which "esteem is enlivened by desire"[34] How possible is this kind of relationship? Who knows? Through all the centuries and in all the different circumstances referred to in this brief history, who can ever know how many couples were bound together by an almost indescribable mixture of love and friendship and devotion? How many thousands or millions of marriages have had this quality but never exposed it to the public in any dramatic way other than in the couple's own steadfast and quiet witness?

But why do we think that we should know about the depth of other people's relationships? We are allowed to see the depth of Abigail and John Adams' love and intimacy because they wrote so well and so honestly to each other, but how many other marriages in history have had similar qualities of companionship and mutual devotion without leaving any written record? Is it naive to suggest that, even as divorce ends many marriages, this tradition of "companionate marriage" in its best sense is still achievable?

I hope it is more than wishful thinking to end this history by holding up this tradition as something more than a dream and to put a painting of Abigail and John Adams in our ever expanding gallery of portraits of marriage. With his starched collar and her ruffled dresses, the picture may not strike us as being very modern, but, knowing what we know about their relationship, who would not want them to be in a prominent place in our collection?

In the sixteenth century, Thomas Cranmer saw that marriage could be something more than what many people of his era experienced or articulated. In the first Book of Common Prayer (1549), Cranmer listed three purposes of marriage. The first two, consistent with the view of marriage that Cranmer inherited, were the "procreation of children" and "remedy against fornication." Not the most exalted notions of matrimony, but honest at least.

But then Cranmer added a third purpose: "mutuall societie, help and comfort." Did he have some insight into the possibility that a marriage could have the qualities of companionship and equality so dramatically lived out by John and Abigail Adams? What a gift this is in our history of marriage. It is documentation for a tradition that can be enormously helpful in our future debates and discussions about marriage.

By the time the Book of Common Prayer was revised for its 1979 edition in the Episcopal Church in the United States, the authors seem to have understood the fact that marriage was undergoing another in its long history of changes. As an honest reflection of the current state of marriage and the fervent hopes for marriage in the late twentieth century, the liturgy for the Celebration and Blessing of Marriage in the American Prayer Book now has the purposes for marriage listed as follows: "The union of husband and wife in heart, body, and mind is intended by God for their mutual joy, for the help and comfort given one another in prosperity and adversity, and, when it is God's will, for the procreation of children and their nurture in the knowledge and love of the Lord."

So Cranmer's purposes of procreation and "help and comfort" are reversed and, interestingly, joy takes the place of "remedy for fornication." Some may say this statement is quite idealistic and that joy may be as fragile a foundation as either "happiness" or "love," but at least this liturgy is honoring the tradition in which "mutuall societie" is at the heart of marriage. A noble tradition that is, and it is achievable if the Adams' letters can be seen as evidence that two human beings can, indeed, be united in "heart, body, and mind."

12

A CONCLUDING MARRIAGE CHECKLIST

I recently saw a pile of books in the home of a young couple who were planning their wedding. On top of the pile was a book entitled *Check List for a Perfect Wedding*. I instinctively recoil from anything that invites "perfection," but I did want to see what was in this book, so I picked it up and opened it. As I browsed through the book, I found that it probably is a helpful guide for those who are planning a fairly elaborate wedding.

At the same time, I knew that I have almost no interest in helping anyone plan a wedding, no matter how "perfect" it might be. What enlivens me is to help people think about marriage—what it has been in the past, what it might be for the couple right now, and how God can be intimately involved in the partnership that is being formed.

This book has been an attempt to see what marriage has been in the past. A fair-minded review of the history of marriage shows that there is no uniform traditional marriage. Instead, there are only "traditions of marriage." I have identified twenty-one of these traditions. Delving deeper into the history of marriage, we might find even more, but, in my analysis, these twenty-one are the "biggies." To summarize them, let's put them into the same form as used in that book about the "perfect wedding." Let's make a checklist of these traditions and then decide which ones our culture no longer values and which ones it does. You may disagree with the way that I check off these traditions, but, based on my reading of Scripture, my understanding of tradition, and my thinking about my own experiences, here is my own checklist (see table "The Traditions of Marriage" on page 100).

As I made my checkmarks, I realized three things: 1) I have reservations about "love" as the basis for marriage, especially if it takes the form of "luv" as discussed in chapter 10; 2) I prefer to see "happiness" as a byproduct of a good marriage, not the goal, as also discussed in chapter 10; and 3) I am less and less convinced that marriage needs to be validated in any official way by an outside authority in order to be a "real marriage."

I did not make my own checklist as a prescriptive recommendation. I simply marked the "Adhered To" column for those traditions that for me as a Christian seem to have the weight of Scripture, tradition, and reason behind them. If this is true, then I think this vision of marriage is appropriate and healthy and holy in my particular culture. I know that others have alternative visions of marriage. A few examples of these alternative visions are as follows:

COMPLETELY SECULAR. Some people do not see marriage as "sacred" and they intentionally avoid having any religious aspects in their weddings. I understand that some people do not perceive marriage to be a "sacred covenant" and therefore would not adhere to that tradition.

SUPERIORITY OF MEN. Some people continue to uphold the superiority of men and the subordination of women in marriage. In 1998, the Southern Baptist Convention amended its official statement of belief to affirm that a wife should "graciously submit to the servant leadership of her husband." At the same time the Southern Baptists were adopting that statement, the Episcopal Church's Executive Council was meeting in Burlington, Vermont.

The Traditions of Marriage

TRADITIONS	ADHERED TO	AMBIGUOUS	NO LONGER ADHERED TO
Endogamy			✓
Polygamy (with concubinage as an option)			✓
Levirate marriage			✓
Arranged marriage (including dowry and "bride price")			✓
Forbidding "mixed marriages" (including miscegenation)			✓
Marriage for political purposes			✓
Marriage for the (sole) purpose of procreation			✓
Marriage transcending class ("No longer slave nor free")	✓		
Celibacy as a vocation	✓		
Women are equal to men	✓		
Lifelong commitment	✓		
Mutual consent	✓		
Outside authority validates the marriage		✓	
Consummation	✓		
Marriage as a secular contract	✓		
Marriage as a sacred covenant	✓		
Betrothal as part of marriage process	✓		
Marrying for love (or "Luv?")		✓	
Marrying for happiness		✓	
Divorce as equivalent to death in ending a marriage	✓		
Marriage for companionship or "mutuall societie"	✓		

Our local newspapers carried several items about how the presiding bishop of the Episcopal Church "gently disagreed" with the Southern Baptist dictum. In that particular case, the checklist of the Baptist Convention and the checklist of the presiding Episcopal bishop would certainly be different.

POLYGAMY. In *Under the Banner of Heaven,* a riveting yet terrifying account of the experiences of people in a fundamentalist Mormon group, Jon Krakauer documents various incidents that occurred in a group where polygamy was retained as a tradition. I am not suggesting that murder and abuse are the inevitable results of polygamous marriages, but Krakauer's book certainly will alarm anyone who cherishes the tradition of equality/mutuality in marriage and who believes that marriage is between two—and only two—people.

NO DIVORCE. Some religious institutions continue to forbid divorce. Only in the twentieth century did the Episcopal Church in the United States pass canonical changes that permit the remarriage of a divorced person whose ex-spouse is still alive. In these changes, the church wrestled with the fact that divorce, while often lamentable, is sometimes necessary. Other people come out very differently on that issue and their checklist would therefore differ from mine.

I do not assume that my views are acceptable to all, but I think a good case can be made for my particular checklist. More important than my own list, though, is the hope that I have been helpful in highlighting the fact that, when it comes to marriage, every person and culture chooses which traditions to adhere to and which to discard, based on the customs and beliefs they have inherited and the understandings they have formed about the human condition. I don't expect people to agree with my checklist in its entirety, but I do hope that people will see that marriage is an ever-changing institution and that any portrait of marriage, including mine, is temporary and will always be a "work in progress."

My main purpose in this book has been educational. I have not written as an advocate for anything other than a fair-minded reading of history. In the debates about marriage that are roiling in our culture, I hope this analysis can move us toward a "level playing field" so debaters can avoid misassumptions and misinformation while resisting prejudice or an overly narrow focus. If any of that has been achieved herein, it will be a blessing and we can praise God from whom all blessings flow.

In the meantime, I think we need to revisit Eden.

13

EDEN REVISITED

Then the Lord God had a trance fall upon the man; and when he had gone to sleep, he took one of his ribs, closing up its place with flesh. The rib which he took from the man the Lord God built up into a woman, and brought her to the man, whereupon the man said,

> "This at last is bone of my bone,
> And flesh of my flesh;
> She shall be called woman,
> For from man was she taken."

(This is why a man leaves his father and mother, and clings to his wife, so that they form one flesh.) (Gen. 2:21–24, The Bible: An American Translation)[35]

I like the this translation, not because of the particular word choices made by the translators, but because of the use of the parentheses around verse 24. To me, the use of parentheses helps to clarify the story. It seems that the person who originally fashioned this story could not resist inserting some editorial comments into the narrative. Apparently the author wanted to connect the ancient story with contemporary customs and therefore added this little parenthetical note. In fact, the primal man did not have a father and mother—if he did, he would not have been the primal man!—and therefore it would be nonsensical for the narrator to suggest that "the man" actually left his father and mother to cling to the woman.

The same thing happens in Genesis 32:32, when, after describing Jacob's wrestling with a mysterious stranger at Peniel, the narrator wrote, "Therefore to this day, the Israelites do not eat the thigh muscle that is on the hip socket, because he struck Jacob on the hip socket at the thigh muscle." As in Genesis 1:24, the narrator rounds off the story with a comment, which could easily be put inside parentheses to indicate that it is an aside to the story. Many good storytellers pause and make a brief personal comment about their story before moving on with the actual narrative.

Whether referring to idiosyncratic eating customs or matrilocal marriage customs (meaning customs that are "located at or centered around the residence of the wife's family or people"), these offhand comments are not critical to the story itself but are interesting little tidbits thrown in by the narrator. If this is a valid way to read the story, then the crux of the Eden story is not about marriage, but about the joy of companionship. The man and woman are "bone of bone" and "flesh of flesh" and there doesn't seem to be anything in the story to prevent us from interpreting this joy as being expressed sexually with an ecstatic whoop from the human being who has found a companion at last.

Some ancient rabbis who commented on this story saw clearly that this scene in Eden is humankind's first sexual experience. In contrast to later Christian interpreters who had a lower regard for the goodness of creation and sexuality, the rabbis were comfortable portraying the primal couple as joyfully clinging to each other in their beautiful nakedness and expressing their joy by doing what comes naturally. Christian commentators, on the other hand, tended to put the sexual spotlight on Genesis 4:1

("Now the man knew his wife Eve, and she conceived and bore Cain") and thereby have the first sexual act occurring after the primal couple has been expelled from the Garden.

By emphasizing the idea that sexual intercourse occurs after the Fall, the common Christian interpretation of the Eden story led to a diminishment of the importance of the joy of sex. The implications of this interpretation for the history of marriage are obvious and have been sketched out in previous chapters. Here, it seems important to revisit the observation made in the first chapter that, in my view, the Hebrew creation stories are not fundamentally about the institution of marriage. Rather, the main thrust of the story is to show two people, leaning on each other (or, in the resonant language of the King James Version of Genesis 2:24, "cleaving" to each other) and trying to make sense of their surroundings, the meaning of their lives, and their relationship to each other and to the God who created them.

Later, procreation and marriage entered the picture, but in the freshness and newness of Eden, the primal couple discovered that their companionship and shared joy with each other was at the heart of creation. To read marriage back into this scene, as the author of Genesis 2:24 did, shifts the emphasis away from the centrality of the couple's experience of companionship and has tended to make marriage into a normative expectation for human life. As one commentator observes, "The surest thing to say about God's intention as recorded in the Genesis material is to say that if we see there the 'institution' of anything at all, it is the 'institution' of an antidote to loneliness."[36]

By clearing away the trappings of marriage from the Eden story, we can see more clearly that humans are meant to be in relationship and community with each other. The forms that this relationship/community take are quite varied. It is easy for those of us who live in the industrialized, individualized West to forget that, for most of recorded history, the word "family" has not meant a "nuclear family" but, instead, has described any group of people who reside together. This model includes the "extended family" in which several generations and many relatives live together and it also includes the tragic reality of "child-headed households" in modern Africa as the HIV-AIDS pandemic eliminates whole generations at once. For the vocal supporters of "traditional families" to focus only on the 1950s American model of "father-mother-two-kids-and-a-dog" is to be overly narrow, quite unhistorical, and often very uncompassionate.

The upshot of this analysis is to invite readers to celebrate the multiplicity of ways that humans find to be companions to one another. Whether single or married or cohabiting or living communally or, as is possible now in the state of Vermont, joined in civil union, human beings from the beginning have sought diverse ways to live in community and to be equal participants in the great adventure of human history.

Lest the phrase "communal living" raise nightmarish visions of rebellious youth doing the things that rebellious youth have always done, let me hasten to say that one of the most profound and sustaining "communal living" experiences that I have had is within the life of a vital and committed Christian congregation. Whether in ancient Rome or Corinth or in contemporary El Salvador or Vermont, a healthy and holy community of Christians can be one icon of the "commonwealth of God" that was begun in Eden, is raised up on earth, and will, I believe, culminate in the reality that God has in store for humankind in eternity.

Can this interpretation help us see that we are all "earthlings" (the translation of Genesis 2:7 proposed by Robert Davidson in *The Cambridge Bible Commentary*[37]) into whom God breathes the breath of life and who are flesh-and-bone companions to each other? I hope so.

As we have seen in this brief history, when basic human companionship has become marriage, it has taken many forms and adhered to many traditions. But if we peel away all the layers of paint that have been added to the original portrait, we are left with a revelation of humankind in all its glory. That glory cannot be pictured in all its fullness or described with any comprehensive adequacy, so there is no portrait that can completely capture the essence of humanness, either in its married or single or communal state.

Artists throughout the ages have given us glimpses of the human condition, sketches of human relationships, and visions of human community, but in the final analysis, we are all in the same situation as those first "earthlings" who leaned on each other and journeyed together as companions. Like them, we work out our salvation with an always unique mixture of joy and "fear and trembling" (Phil. 2:12) even as we are guided and nourished by God and "surrounded by so great a cloud of witnesses" as we "run with perseverance the race that is set before us" (Heb. 12:1).

I hope the portraits in this book give us a bit of insight into how our ancestors have coped with their journeys, especially the journey of marriage. We all continue to be called to paint our own portraits and live out our own lives in relationship to each other and to the God who created us in Edenic glory, who continually seeks to redeem us and bring us into right relationship, and who sustains us with grace and truth.

EPILOGUE

Sketches for a New Portrait of Marriage

As I muse about where church and society's conceptions and practices of marriage are headed, I have a vision. It is not crystal clear or fully formed. It is more of a series of sketches than a completed portrait. Here is what those sketches look like at the moment:

Two people meet. They gradually get to know each other and experience each other in good times and bad. They each see flaws in the other, but are ineluctably drawn together because of the joy they share and the future they envision with each other. Their family and friends are generally supportive of the relationship between these two people and genuinely hope it will last. The partners in this relationship come from different religious traditions, but have found a congregation that welcomes them, nourishes them, and has them involved in a special mission project that is an important part of their life together.

For more than a year, these two people grow closer and closer to each other and realize they want their relationship to be permanent. They light-heartedly disagree about the exact moment when each of them knew they wanted to make a lasting commitment, but it is clear to both of them that the reality of their relationship is as substantial as anything they have ever experienced.

When they both agree that the time has arrived to make a formal commitment to each other, they make a plan to go to the local courthouse to get a civil union license. This license, once it is signed by them and witnessed by a public official, will create a legal bond between them. The two of them will be entitled to all of the rights guaranteed by the state and federal government and they will be able to put all their property into joint ownership. In addition, they are assured that in case of serious illness, it will be their partner who has the primary role in making decisions about medical care. In case of death, the survivor will receive all the benefits that have been arranged through pension and insurance plans. A further aspect of the couple's civil union status will be the joint responsibility they will have for children they produce or adopt.

Getting the civil union license is a big step for the couple. They are not taking this step lightly or unadvisedly. They certainly are not getting the license on a sudden impulse. They planned the event for quite a while and invited family and friends to join them in a celebration. On the day of their being united in civil union, they arrange to have a justice of the peace meet them in a small public room at the court house.

Their parents, two siblings, and three of their closest friends (one of whom had introduced the partners to each other) come with the couple to the courthouse. The small entourage goes to the town clerk's office. The couple obtains and pays for the license, then they take it into the adjoining room where the justice of the peace is waiting. The ceremony is brief but poignant. There is laughter. There are tears. A small bottle of champagne is uncorked. The couple invites the justice of the peace to join them in a toast.

A few minutes later, the happy people leave the courthouse and pile into their cars. They drive to the reception hall that has been rented for the occasion. As soon as the couple walks in, there is raucous and sustained applause as they make their way down the long red carpet that had been placed on the floor earlier that afternoon. On a long table at the other end of the room is a huge cake, flanked by an extensive array of photos. There are photos of each of them as newborn babies, as school children, and as high school graduates holding fiercely to their diplomas. Other pictures show them together: on a hike, splashing in the ocean, lounging on a couch, and kissing under some mistletoe. One of their friends who had accompanied them to the courthouse goes to the table and adds one more photo that has just been taken. It shows the couple looking on as the justice of the peace signs their civil union license.

Before the cake is cut, the partners stand together while many guests give short testimonials about the couple or share wishes and hopes for the couple's future. There is much laughter and not a few tears. Finally, when everyone has finished making comments, the partners go to the microphone, thank the guests for joining them, and then kiss to enthusiastic applause. After that, they cut the cake, nod to the musicians in the corner, and go to the middle of the hall to dance the first of what would be many dances as the evening and the party progress.

One of the guests at the party is the pastor of the congregation that has become important to the couple as their relationship deepened. The pastor thoroughly enjoys the festivities and even dances a few times before the party ends.

A few weeks afterward, the couple meets with the pastor for another in their series of many counseling sessions. Over the course of several months, the pastor helps them discuss with each other the meaning of marriage, their experiences in their families of origin, and the dynamics of the relationship to which they are now committed. In addition to these counseling sessions, the couple has the opportunity to meet with other couples in the congregation, who share stories and reflections about the joys and sorrows and comforts and challenges of their own marriages.

Toward the end of the counseling process, the pastor convenes a group of parishioners to meet with the couple. The group consists of people who are young and old, single and married, widowed and divorced. What they have in common is that they have come to know the couple and feel they can speak honestly and lovingly about what they perceive in the couple's relationship. There is much laughter and not a few tears. The partners come away from the meeting with a powerful feeling of support and some clear ideas about a few goals that will be important for them to pursue in the future.

A few weeks later, at the main Sunday worship service, the couple is seated in their usual place, in a pew about halfway back on the left side. The service begins as usual, with a hymn, an opening prayer, Scripture readings, and another hymn. Then, before the sermon, the pastor calls the couple forward so they can make some initial promises about their commitment to their faith, to the congregation, and to each other. After that, the partners sit in the front row while the pastor preaches a sermon based on the Scripture readings for the day but includes some reflections on the meaning of marriage and on the relationship of the two people who have just come forward.

Following the sermon, the couple joins the pastor in front of the altar. The pastor asks the people in the congregation if they will support this couple in their life together and receives a surprisingly loud and heartfelt "We will!" The partners then face each other, speak their vows, and exchange rings. The pastor blesses them. They embrace and go into the congregation to exchange greetings of peace. That part of the liturgy takes much longer than usual because every person in the congregation wants to greet them.

Finally, the couple returns to their usual place and the service continues. The coffee hour that day is particularly festive. On a table set up along one wall are all the photos that had been on display at the party many months before, but now a new picture is added. One of the ushers had snapped some Polaroid photos of the couple at the altar with the pastor. The best one has been put into a frame and is sitting in a prominent place on the table.

Observers who look at what is sketched above will quickly notice several things.

First, and, of course, controversially, I never referred to the two key people as "man and woman" or "husband and wife." They are simply "the couple" or "the partners." In my vision, the important thing is the "twoness," not the "maleness and femaleness," that matters. When it comes to leaning on each other and trying to figure out the meaning of life, how to live together, and two people's relationship to each other and to God, the key is not gender but truthfulness, mutuality, and faithfulness. Two men or two women can make that commitment to each other just as well as a man and a woman can.

My purpose in this sketch is not to sneak in the topic of "gay marriage" at the very end and then quickly depart. Rather, in coming to the conclusion of this work, I am led to see that the trajectory of the history of marriage brings us inevitably to this matter. I have listed in the bibliography some of the books and articles that I have found useful in forming my own views on this new development in the history of marriage. In the sketch I have made here, I am simply hoping to show that it is reasonable and consistent with the history of marriage to welcome our gay brothers in Christ and our lesbian sisters in Christ into matrimonial equality.

Besides the inclusion of same-gender relationships in my sketch, I also envision a situation that has some other new features.

In my vision, there is a very clear separation between the role of the civil institution and the role of the religious institution. In what I have sketched, the civil authorities do what they have always done, which is to be concerned about property, legality, and the welfare of children. The religious community, on the other hand, does what it can do best—counsel, support, celebrate, and bless. Each "does its own thing" and there is no mixing up of who is doing what. The pastor does not sign a license and the justice of the peace does not try to import any religiosity.

Speaking from my own experience, I grow increasingly impatient with the expectation that I serve as a government official in signing civil marriage licenses. I don't sign civil birth certificates, but I do have the honor of officiating at baptisms. I don't sign civil death certificates, but I do have the privilege of officiating at memorial services. Why, in the case of marriage, am I asked to function in the dual role of civil authority and religious authority? It makes no sense, other than the convenience of "one-stop shopping," and it makes for a great deal of confusion. I am eager for the day when these two roles are clearly separated.

As a corollary to the separation of civil and religious roles, I envision a situation in which all partners, including heterosexual couples, get a civil union license when they are ready to enter into a secular contract with each other. For some people, that would be sufficient. Whether they ever seek the support and blessing of a religious institution is irrelevant to their being joined in civil union. Once a couple has that license, they are legally joined and have all the responsibilities and rights that flow from that civil union.

In my sketch, I did not use the word "marriage" until the couple got to their counseling sessions with the pastor. Obviously, that part of this vision will cause great consternation with many people. Isn't this restriction of the words "marriage" to a relationship that is supported and blessed by a religious institution depriving nonreligious people of something they want (that is, a social "stamp of approval")? That's one way to look at it. Another is to shift to a new paradigm and envision a society in which "civil union" is exactly the stamp of approval that all couples would get when they enter into a legal commitment to each other. In that paradigm, no couple gets anything different from any other couple. In a democratic society or a fair-minded religious institution, what could be a more commendable achievement?

In my vision, people for whom the "M" word has deep and sacred meaning are welcome to receive the blessing of their particular religious institution. Once the couple has prepared for the blessing of their relationship and has received genuine support and encouragement from the people who share their spiritual journey, they are, in the eyes of that congregation (but probably not in the eyes of some other congregations), "married." If those who desire to be married happen to be gay or lesbian people, bisexual or transgender, they will not be welcome in some religious institutions, but they will be warmly welcomed in others. If some people refuse to honor the committed relationship of two men or two women, then they are not forced to do so. But in the meantime, partners who want to commit themselves to a life of fidelity and mutuality with each other can do so in the midst of their faith community.

By separating the civil and religious roles, we could create an intriguing new possibility: if, for a variety of reasons, the couple either cannot or prefer not to get a civil union license (for example, a widow and a widower who cannot make the economic sacrifice of giving up their Social Security benefits from their former marriages), I see no reason why they should not be able to seek the support and blessing of their religious community. Why should a relationship that clearly manifests faithfulness, commitment, and mutuality be relegated to "second-class status" just because it is not a legal contract? A couple may not want or need a civil union, but may earnestly desire and deserve to live in "holy union" with the support of their religious community. Why stand in their way?

In the vision portrayed above, I refrained from any mention of the theological realities that are of great importance to me. "God" and "Jesus" and "Spirit" are not part of my sketch. I do this not to dodge these fundamental issues, but rather to be sure that there is room for many couples in this vision. If I happened to be the pastor in a situation like the one sketched above, then I certainly would be inviting the couple to ponder deeply and steadfastly how God, Jesus, and the Spirit are at the center of their life together.

This seems to be a good place to end. From my point of view, once we have invoked the presence of God-as-Trinity, there's not much more to be said. I hope what I have written here is sufficient to help some people look clearly at the history of marriage and consider the future of marriage with an open mind and an open heart.

APPENDIX A

Questions for Reflection and Discussion

BEFORE READING THE BOOK

What is your definition of traditional marriage?

In what ways do you think the institution of marriage has changed in the past hundred years?

Can you identify any marriage traditions that you are glad have disappeared from our culture?

CHAPTER ONE

If you were going to write a creation story, how would it begin and how would you portray the first humans?

CHAPTER TWO

In your experience, what corresponds to the ancient concept of "tribe?" How does your view of marriage relate to that experience?

What do you think of polygamy? If you are male, how might your thinking be different if you were female, and vice versa?

What kind of "mixed marriages" do you see as being problematic? Why?

CHAPTER THREE

What are some contemporary examples of the intersection of marriage and politics? How do you think those have worked out?

CHAPTER FOUR

On a scale of 1 (not very important) to 10 (very important), how would you rate the importance of procreation in terms of the purpose of marriage? Why?

CHAPTER FIVE

What celibate people have you known? What influence have they had on your perspective on human relationships?

"Women are equal to men"—what do you think?

How has divorce affected your life? How important is lifelong commitment in marriage? How realistic is that expectation?

CHAPTER SIX

Beyond "mutual consent," what else do you think is necessary for the validation of marriage? Why?

CHAPTERS SEVEN AND EIGHT

What do you think is the role of the state and the role of religious institutions in modern marriage? What changes would you like to see in this area?

CHAPTER NINE

How would a more formal tradition of betrothal have changed your experience of family and/or marriage?

CHAPTER TEN

How would you compare "love" to "luv?" Is that a helpful distinction? Why or why not?

On a scale of 1 (not very important) to 10 (very important), how would you rate the importance of "happiness" in a marriage? How would you explain your rating?

CHAPTER ELEVEN

Describe and name an example of a couple whom you perceive as having established a marriage of "mutuall societie?" Would that couple agree?

CHAPTER TWELVE

Which of the twenty-one traditions of marriage identified in this book do you think we should continue to adhere to? Which ones should not be adhered to? Which ones are you less clear about?

CHAPTER THIRTEEN

If you could interview the primal couple, what would you ask them?

EPILOGUE

What would be essential in your sketch for a portrait of marriage?

What other metaphors, instead of "portraits," might you use to help someone understand the history of marriage?

When someone says, "Marriage is between one man and one woman," what do you say in response?

What is your definition of "traditional marriage"? Has it changed now that you have considered the various traditions of marriage dealt with in this book? If so, what accounts for your changed perspective?

APPENDIX B

Marriage Quiz

A POP QUIZ ON MARRIAGE
by Stephanie Coontz[38]

True or false?
(Answers begin on the following page.)

1. Women are more eager to marry than men.
2. Men are threatened by women who are their intellectual and occupational equals, preferring to be with much younger, less accomplished women.
3. There are more long-term marriages today than in the past.
4. Americans have become much more tolerant of all sexual activity.
5. The growth in the number of couples living together and even having children without formal marriage ceremonies or licenses reflects a sharp break with centuries-old tradition.
6. Educated married women are increasingly "opting out" of work to stay home with their children.
7. Men and women who hold nontraditional views about gender roles are less likely to marry and more likely to divorce than those with traditional values.

8. Divorce rates in the 1950s were lower than at any other time in the twentieth century.
9. Throughout history, philosophers and theologians have always believed that strong marital commitments form the foundation of a virtuous society.
10. American women have more positive attitudes toward marriage than Japanese women do.
11. Divorce has always been a disaster for women and children.
12. The preferred form of marriage through the ages has been between one man and one woman.
13. Born-again Christians are just as likely to divorce as more secular Americans.

Answers

1. FALSE. From 1970 to the late 1990s, men's attitudes toward marriage became more favorable, while women's became less so. By the end of the century, more men than women said that marriage was their ideal lifestyle. And on average, men became more content with their marriage over time, while women grew less so. A majority of divorced men and women report that the wife was the one who wanted out of the marriage. A recent study of divorces that occurred after age 40 found that wives initiated two-thirds of them.

2. FALSE. The difference in ages of men and women at first marriage has been narrowing for the past 80 years and is now at a historic low. By the end of he 1990s, 39 percent of women age 35 to 44 lived with younger men. Men still rate youth and good looks higher than women do when looking for a mate, but those criteria no longer outweigh all others. Men are much more likely now to seek a mate who has the same level of education and similar earnings potential. College-educated women are more likely to marry and less likely to divorce than women with less education.

3. TRUE. Although divorce rates have risen, death rates have fallen even more steeply, so that more couples will celebrate their 40th wedding anniversaries now than at any time in the past. Furthermore, the divorce rate reached its height more than 21 years ago. It has fallen by more than 25 percent since 1981.

4. FALSE. Americans are now more tolerant of consenting sexual relations between unmarried adults than in the past. But surveys show that disapproval of adultery, sexual coercion, rape, and sex with minors has increased over the past 30 years and is now at a historic high. In 1889, a girl could legally consent to sex at 10, 11, or 12 in half the states, and in Delaware the age of consent was 7. There were many more prostitutes per capita in late 19th century America than there are today—resulting in high incidence of venereal disease among respectably married women infected by their husbands.

5. FALSE. For the first thousand years of its existence, the church held that a marriage was valid if a couple claimed they had exchanged words of consent—even if there were no witnesses and no priest to officiate. Not until 1754 did England require issuance of a license for marriage to be valid. Informal marriage and cohabitation were so common in early 19th century America that one judge estimated that one-third of all children were born to couples who were not legally married.

6. FALSE. The likelihood that college-educated women will drop out of the labor force because of having children declined by half from 1984 to 2004. And among all mothers with children under 6, the most highly educated are the least likely to leave their jobs, with that likelihood declining with each level of educational attainment.

7. TRICK QUESTION. Women with nontraditional values are indeed more likely to divorce than women with traditional views, but they are also more likely to get married in the first place. As for men, those with traditional values about

gender are more likely to marry than nontraditional men, but they are more likely to divorce. We don't precisely know why this discrepancy exists, but it probably has something to do with the fact that women's views on gender are changing more rapidly than men's.

8. FALSE. Aside from a huge spike in divorce immediately after World War II, divorce rates in the 1950s were higher than in any previous decade aside from the Depression, and almost one in three marriages formed in the 1950s eventually ended in divorce. Divorce rates rose steadily from the 1890s through the 1960s (with a dip in the Depression and a spike after World War II), soared in the 1970s, and have fallen since 1981. Marriage rates, however, have also fallen significantly in the past 25 years.

9. FALSE. Ancient Roman philosophers and medieval theologians thought that loving your spouse too much was a form of "adultery," a betrayal of one's obligations to country or God. The ancient Greeks held that the purest form of love was between two men. In China, Confucian philosophers ranked the relationship between husband and wife as second from the bottom of their list of the most important family ties, with the father–elder son relationship topping the list. Early Christians thought marriage was inescapably tainted by the presence of sex. According to the medieval church, virgins ranked highest in godliness, widows were second, and wives a distant third.

10. TRUE. In 2001 schoolgirls around the world were asked whether they agreed with the statement that everyone needed to marry. Three-quarters of American schoolgirls agreed. But in Japan, 88 percent of schoolgirls disagreed.

11. FALSE. Divorce in modern America often does cause a sharp drop in the economic standard of living for women and children. But states that legalized no-fault divorce experienced an average 20 percent decline in suicide rates among married women over the following five years. And a recent study suggests that while divorce worsens the emo-

tional well-being of 55 percent to 60 percent of children, it improves the well-being of 40 to 45 percent.

12. FALSE. The form of marriage that has been approved by more societies than any other through the ages has been polygamy—one man and many women. That family form is the one mentioned most often in the first five books of the Bible. In some societies, one woman could marry several men. In others, two families could forge an alliance by marrying off a son or daughter to the "ghost" of the other family's dead child. For most of history, the main impetus for marriage was getting in-laws and managing property, not love or sex.

13. TRUE. Thirty-five percent of born-again Christians in this country have divorced, almost the same as the 37 percent of atheists and agnostics who have divorced—and 23 percent of born-again Christians have divorced twice. Among Pentecostals, the divorce rate is more than 40 percent. The region with the highest divorce rate is the Bible belt.

NOTES

1. E. J. Graff, *What is Marriage For?* (Boston: Beacon Press, 2004), 2.
2. Judith Romney Wegner, *Chattel or Person? The Status of Women in the Mishnah* (New York: Oxford University Press, 1988), 13.
3. *Webster's New Collegiate Dictionary* (Springfield, Mass.: G & C. Merriam Co., 1956), 537.
4. Graff, *What is Marriage For?*, 153.
5. Stephanie Coontz, *Marriage: A History* (New York: Viking, 2005), 256.
6. Mike Anton, "Marriage a Malleable Institution throughout History," History News Network, Seattle, April 1, 2004.
7. Joan Comay, *Who's Who in the Old Testament*, vol. 1 in *Who's Who in the Bible* (New York: Bonanza Books, 1980), 360–61.
8. Christopher L. Webber, *Re-Inventing Marriage: A Re-View and Re-Vision* (Harrisburg, Pa.: Morehouse Publishing, 1994), 28.
9. *To Set Our Hope on Christ* (New York: Office of Communication, the Episcopal Church Center, 2005), 127.
10. Paul D. Hanson, *The People Called: The Growth of Community in the Bible* (San Francisco: Harper & Row, 1987), 469–70.
11. Webber, *Re-Inventing Marriage*, 79.
12. John Oxenham, "In Christ There Is No East or West," 1913.
13. Graff, *What is Marriage For?*, 60–61.
14 Nick Page, *The Tabloid Bible* (Louisville: Westminster John Knox Press, 1998), 9.

15. Lawrence Stone, *The Family, Sex, and Marriage in England 1500–1800* (New York: Harper & Row, 1977), 55.
16. Philip Lyndon Reynolds, *Marriage in the Western Church: The Christianization of Marriage During the Patristic and Early Medieval Periods* (New York: E.J. Brill, 1994), 332.
17. Theodore Tappert, ed., trans., *Luther's Works*, vol. 54, *Table Talk* (Philadelphia: Fortress Press, 1967), 363.
18. Theodore Mackin, *What is Marriage?* (New York: Paulist Press, 1982), 51.
19. *Webster's New Collegiate Dictionary*, 912.
20. Adrian Thatcher, *Living Together and Christian Ethics* (Cambridge, UK: Cambridge University Press, 2002), 122.
21. Loretta Lynn, "The Pill" © 1975 Loretta Lynn.
22. Graff, *What is Marriage For?*, 221.
23. *The Proper for the Lesser Feasts and Fasts, 1997* (New York: Church Publishing, 1998), 292.
24. Ibid.
25. Ibid.
26. Lyrics from "Our Town" by Sammy Cahn and Jimmy Van Heusen, 1955, quoted in *Reading Lyrics*, ed. Robert Gottlieb and Robert Kimball (New York: Pantheon Books, 2000), 478.
27. David R. Shumway, *Modern Love: Romance, Intimacy, and the Marriage Crisis* (New York: New York University Press, 2003), 12.
28. Douglas John Hall, *Why Christian? For Those on the Edge of Faith* (Minneapolis: Fortress Press, 1998), 112.
29. Pamela Paul, interview in *People Weekly* 57/11 (March 25, 2002), 119.
30. Graff, *What is Marriage For?*, 234.
31. Richard P. McBrien, referring to *1983 Code of Canon Law*, in his book *Catholicism* (San Francisco: Harper Collins Publishers, 1994), 796.
32. Richard Pryor, as quoted by Robert Byrne in *The 1,911 Best Things Anyone Ever Said* (New York: Fawcett Columbine, 1988), 296.
33. Frank Shuffleton, ed. *The Letters of John and Abigail Adams* (New York: Penguin Books, 2004).
34. Jean H. Hagstrum, *Esteem Enlivened by Desire: The Couple from Homer to Shakespeare* (Chicago: University of Chicago Press, 1992).
35. J. M. Powis Smith, ed., *The Bible: An American Translation* (Chicago: University of Chicago Press, 1931), 6.
36. Willim Seth Adams, "Established by God in Creation," in *With Ever Joyful Hearts: Essays in Liturgy and Music Honoring Marion*

J. Hatchett, ed. J. Neil Alexander (New York: Church Publishing, 1999), 205.

37. Robert Davidson, *Genesis 1–11*, in *The Cambridge Bible Commentary* (Cambridge, UK: Cambridge University Press, 1973), 31.

38. Stephanie Coontz, "A Pop Quiz on Marriage," *New York Times*, op-ed, Sunday, February 19, 2006.

BIBLIOGRAPHY

Adams, William Seth. "Established by God in Creation": Were Adam and Eve Really 'Married'?" In *With Ever Joyful Hearts: Essays on Liturgy and Music Honoring Marion J. Hatchett*, ed. J. Neil Alexander. New York: Church Publishing, 1999.

Anderson, Gary. "Celibacy or Consummation in the Garden? Reflections on Early Jewish and Christian Interpretations of the Garden of Eden." *Harvard Theological Review* 82/2 (April 1989).

Anton, Mike. "Marriage a Malleable Institution Throughout History." History News Network. Seattle, April 1, 2004.

Argyle, A. W. "Wedding Customs at the Time of Jesus." *The Espository Times* 86/7 (April 1975).

Bennison, Charles. "Some Chronological Benchmarks in the History of Social and Ecclesiastical Opinion Regarding Sexuality and Marriage." Paper delivered at a conference at Episcopal Divinity School, Cambridge, Massachusetts, June 24, 1993.

Bevington, David. "The Difficult Idea of Companionate Marriage." *The Journal of Religion* 74/3 (July 1994).

Coontz, Stephanie. "A Pop Quiz on Marriage." *New York Times*. Op-Ed. February 19, 2006.

Coontz, Stephanie. *Marriage: a History: From Obedience to Intimacy, or How Love Conquered Marriage*. New York: Viking Penguin, 2005.

Cott, Nancy. *Public Vows: A History of Marriage and the Nation*. Cambridge: Harvard University Press, 2000.

Crysdale, Cynthia S.W. "Christian Marriage and Homosexual Monogamy." *Our Selves, Our Souls, and Bodies.* Boston: Cowley Publications, 1996.

Ellison, Marvin. *Same Sex Marriage.* Cleveland: Pilgrim Press, 2004.

Freedman, Estelle B. "Boston Marriage, Free Love, and Fictive Kin: Historical Alternatives to Mainstream Marriage." *Organization of American Historians Newsletter* 32/3 (August 2004).

Gaechter, Paul. "The Chronology from Mary's Betrothal to the Birth of Christ." *Theological Studies* 2/2 (May 1941).

Graff, E. J. *What is Marriage For?* Boston: Beacon Press, 2004.

Gudorf. Christine E. "Sexual Pleasure as Grace and Gift." *The Other Side* 34/3 (May/June 1998).

Hagstrum, Jean H. *Esteem Enlivened by Desire: The Couple from Homer to Shakespeare.* Chicago: University of Chicago Press, 1992.

Hartog, Hendrik. *Man and Wife in America: A History.* Cambridge: Harvard University Press, 2000.

Haslett, Adam. "Love Supreme," *The New Yorker* (May 31, 2004).

Krakauer, Jon. *Under the Banner of Heaven: A Story of Violent Faith.* New York: Anchor Books, 2004.

Lloyd, Jennifer M. "Conflicting Expectations in Nineteenth-Century British Matrimony: The Failed Companionate Marriage of Effie Gray and John Ruskin." *Journal of Women's History* 11/2 (Summer 1999).

Mackin, Theodore. *What Is Marriage?* New York: Paulist Press, 1982.

Marquardt, Elizabeth (interviewed). "No Good Divorce." *The Christian Century* (February 2006).

Metha, Monica. "The Myth of Marriage." www.alternet.org/story/23400. July 21, 2005.

Palmer, Paul F, "Christian Marriage: Contract or Covenant?" *Theological Studies* 33 (1972).

Paul, Pamela. *The Starter Marriage and the Future of Matrimony.* New York: Villard 2002.

"Report of the Task Force on the Blessing of Persons Living in Same-Gender Relationships," June 8, 2004 (available from the Diocesan Office of the Episcopal Diocese of Vermont, 5 Rock Point Road, Burlington, Vermont 05401-2735).

Reynolds, Philip Lyndon. *Marriage in the Western Church: The Christianization of Marriage during the Patristic and Early Medieval Periods.* New York: E.J. Brill, 1994.

Scott, Kieran, and Michael Warren, eds., *Perspectives on Marriage: A Reader*. New York: Oxford University Press, 2001.

Shumway, David R. *Modern Love: Romance, Intimacy, and the Marriage Crisis*. New York: New York University Press, 2003.

"State of the Union: The Marriage Issue," *The Nation* 279/1 (July 5, 2004).

Stone, Lawrence. *The Family, Sex, and Marriage in England 1500–1800*. New York: Harper & Row, 1977.

Temple, Gray. *Gay Unions: In the Light of Scripture, Tradition, and Reason*. New York: Church Publishing, 2004.

Thatcher, Adrian. *Living Together and Christian Ethics*. Cambridge, UK: Cambridge University Press, 2002.

Thatcher, Adrian. "When Does Christian Marriage Begin?" *The Witness* (April 2000).

Webber, Christopher L. *Re-Inventing Marriage: A Re-View and Re-Vision*. Harrisburg, Pa.: Morehouse Publishing, 1994.

Wegner, Judith Romney. *Chattel or Person? The Status of Women in the Mishnah*. New York: Oxford University Press, 1988.

Westermarck, Edward. *The History of Human Marriage*. New York: Allerton Book Co., 1922.

Witte, John. *From Sacrament to Contract: Marriage, Religion, and Law in the Western Tradition*. Westminster John Knox Press, 1997.

Wood, Gordon S. "Pursuits of Happiness," *The New Republic* (April 12, 2004).

Wylie-Kellerman, Jeanie, and Julie Wortman, eds., "Holy Matrimony," *The Witness* 78/12 (December 1995).

Yalom, Marilyn. *A History of the Wife*. New York: Harper Collins, 2001.